AUTHOR	CLASS
CUTTER, V.	G3
TITLE Go East young man	No
	485114898

D1144750

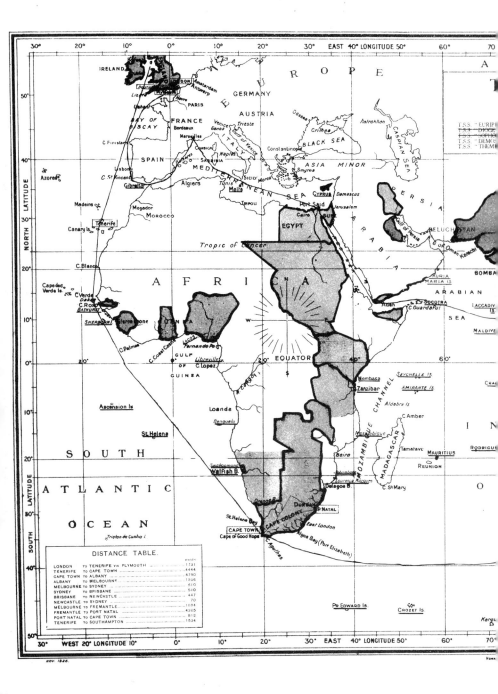

DISTANCE TABLE.

		KNOTS
LONDON	TO TENERIFE VIA PLYMOUTH	1731
TENERIFE	TO CAPE TOWN	4444
CAPE TOWN	TO ALBANY	4790
ALBANY	TO MELBOURNE	1806
MELBOURNE	TO SYDNEY	580
SYDNEY	TO BRISBANE	510
BRISBANE	TO NEWCASTLE	447
NEWCASTLE	TO SYDNEY	70
MELBOURNE	TO FREMANTLE	1684
FREMANTLE	TO PORT NATAL	4365
PORT NATAL	TO CAPE TOWN	812
TENERIFE	TO SOUTHAMPTON	1534

Go East Young Man

★ ★ ★

V. CUTTER

Foreword by Michael Grey, C.B.E., T.D., D.L.

Regency Press (London & New York) Ltd.
125 High Holborn, London WC1V 6QA

To
My Father

ISBN 0 7212 0770 7

Printed and bound in Great Britain by
Buckland Press Ltd., Dover, Kent.

Contents

Acknowledgements

My thanks to members of the family and to friends and aquaintances of my father who have provided me with recollections of the past. Also to Miss Fairey and Miss Fluck of 'Craven Books' for their encouragement and interest in the conception of this book.

Val Cutter

List of Illustrations

John Hindley, Senior.

Foreword

Although he was ten years my senior, I knew John Hindley well, and remember with pleasure his quiet undemonstrative personality. Like him, I also spent an adult working life of well over forty years in the absorbing, exasperating and diminishing Lancashire textile industry.

To those who are old enough to recall the times in which John Hindley made his journey and wrote his diary and letters these pages will evoke fascinating memories in more than one dimension. To the younger reader they will seem almost as remote as ancient history from today's world.

It was the Lancashire textile industry which took John Hindley on his travels. Even though it had already started to decline by 1927 from the peak it had reached during the earlier part of the century, the Lancashire textile industry was still a massive force in British export trade and one of the great industrial employers of labour. The fate which has since befallen it, reducing it to near extinction, was still in the future and unsuspected. That fate was a combination of the bitter flowering of the seeds of its own destruction which lay hidden in the structure of its former greatness—and the feeble indifference to that fate shown by successive post-war British Governments and the civil servants who advised them.

The next dimension was that of travel. In 1927 Lindberg had just made his historic transatlantic flight, but the pioneering inter-continental flights of Amy Johnson, Jim Mollison and their adventurous contemporaries still lay in the future. The neurotic bustle of commercial air travel was yet to come and major journeys lasted days and weeks rather than hours, and most were made in enforced leisure by railway or steamship.

In those days also the school atlas still showed vast tracts of the world coloured in imperial red. The world could be encircled without setting foot anywhere the Union Jack did not fly. A few years later King George V was to say in one of the early Christmas broadcasts "under the British Flag so many millions eat their daily bread with none to make them afraid." No doubt today, those who specialise in the sour task of rewriting history to suit the modern taste for debunking would pick all sorts of holes in that royal sentiment. But it was a truth which was also part of the background to John Hindley's travels.

In 1927 the "war to end all wars" had itself ended only nine years before and the world was still relaxing in the relief; even if the post-war boom in which Lancashire textiles had amply shared was petering out, the Great Depression was still unsuspected. Mussolini had bobbed to the surface in Italy, though he seemed little more than a buffoon. Hitler was still unheard of outside Germany. Alfonso XIII was on the throne of Spain whose civil war was still a decade in the future. The League of Nations still seemed something to be believed in and was endlessly busy in its attempts to settle the affairs of Europe. Japan had not yet launched itself into Manchuria, and the world seemed a calmer, safer and more rational place than anyone was ever to know again.

These then were the background circumstances which John Hindley made his journeys and in which he wrote his diaries and letters. We are left wondering what further experiences there were from Delhi onwards, why the records ceased so abruptly, and what was the degree of success for the business of his firm. And one small last thought—did young Reg ever get that Rhino hide, and if so what did he do with it?

All in all this book reveals a fascinating mixture of some rather callow comments by a young man on his first major foray abroad, amply leavened by many deep and perceptive thoughts and observations about the wide world in which he was travelling. We shall not see its like again; there is no time for this sort of business-cum-pleasure journeying in the hectic world of today.

Michael Grey

Former Chairman of the U.K. Textile Manufacturers Association;
and Member of The Cotton Board (later The Textile Council).

Introduction

This book is based on the diary of a young man who travelled to the East. Most of the countries through which he travelled were then part of the British Empire, and the year in which he set off from England was 1927. The diary was written over a nine-month period, and together with his collection of photographs, letters, postcards and other items, give an exact record of how a young man from a comfortable middle-class background saw the world in the 1920s. The journey included travel in South Africa, Australia, New Zealand and the Far East, also a three-week train journey through India.

The diarist was able to paint a vivid and accurate picture in those days of all he saw and heard, simply because he would have a few preconceived ideas as to what places would be like, or how he would find things. Written before the days of television, travel brochures or mass advertising the descriptive passages would be naturally more spontaneous. But perhaps more remarkable was the apparent ease of travel for someone of adequate means: there is hardly need for a passport, there is no mention of visas or of inoculations, and there is only one mention of health check—which is on disembarking in Australia. The custom of buying one's own bedding before setting out on a long-distance train journey in India, and of engaging and paying the fare of a bearer, were just starting to die out; as John finds to his cost.

The slowness of travel by steamship was a mixed blessing, and passengers had to make their own entertainment. The classic shipboard romance is there: but also passengers had a lot more time to tire of one another.

It was partly for business purposes that the trip was made, and was with regard to trading in textiles. The following extract by a writer of these times is most salutary to the would-be exporter, in the chapter headed "From Lancashire to Asia" it reads: "Slowness of travel is another great disadvantage to the Englishman trying to show his samples in Asia. Steamship travel from Great Britain takes over six weeks; the Japanese can have samples (of cloth) from Australia shipped home copied and exported back in this time."

Unfortunately, when John Hindley set off to travel on his own to the Far East, lack of time and the distractions of Shanghai did not allow him enough time to visit Japan: but the remarks about the threat of the Japaneses at the time to the British textile trade, had been already recorded in his diary.

Background

It is now some ten years since my father, John Hindley, died; and recently I have felt that the moment was right to read—for the first time—his diary, which I knew vaguely to be of some 'World Trip' which he had travelled as a young man. Three albums of photographs of South Africa, Australia, and New Zealand together with his letters home, have recently come to light: I can remember seeing some remarkable black and white film of Southern India taken from the train—but unfortunately this cine-film is now mislaid.

Luckily the personal letters which he wrote to immediate members of the family were kept and returned to him when he got home. There were also long typed summary letters which I presume were sent back to the Mill to be read and filed, or else put on to the dictaphone (a new invention of the time which he was very fond of using). These typed letters were very detailed, and much of the information about current prices and styles of cloth have been omitted.

★ ★ ★

My first task then, was to find out why this particular journey was made, and how it was that the diary came to be written.

The separate firms of Hindley Bros. and V. E. Haighton, were two of the many textile producers classed as cotton manufacturers who had set up in Lancashire in the town of Nelson during the very early part of this century. This was a thriving town at the time, and was traditionally weaving fine cotton fabrics, and a fine woollen cloth called Zephyr.

With the decline of the British influence over her trade within the Empire, much of the export trade of the textile manufacturers was waning, and her vast cotton trade was being lost. By 1927 things were changing rapidly in the world, and the trade with India had almost disappeared. Both firms had a considerable number of business contacts with South Africa, and more particularly with Australia, and it was to this part of the world that they decided to pay some attention. Vernie Haighton was setting out to travel these countries, in order to find out about the state of the trade, and to seek orders. It seems that Vernie also had intentions of setting up in another side of the textile trade subsequent to his travels. John Hindley was his nephew, and was just twenty-one, so it was convenient for them to travel together for part of the way.

From John Hindley's point of view the trip had a double purpose; one was to learn something of the textile trade abroad, particularly as to what the customer demand was: the other intention was to have something of a holiday and to see the world.

It was very much in John's character to keep such a diary—although he had not been known to ever keep a diary before or since this particular time. He was a quiet, serious and observant young man. The fare had been paid for by his eldest brother as a twenty-first birthday present, and he probably felt somewhat duty bound to report back fully about business affairs to his benefactor. Having made a determined start to keep this diary, it seems that John found an ability as well as a certain enjoyment in putting his thoughts on paper after his somewhat stilted beginnings.

*   *   *

The ramifications of the textile industry are vast, but it might be helpful to the reader of the diary to understand a little of the environment in which the business was carried out. Similarly the family with its large age gaps and intermarriage, was somewhat complex. I therefore limited my quest for background information to what was going on in Nelson around the time that the diary was written, something about t'mill, and only the members of the family to whom letters were addressed. Even this comparatively small task proved far more difficult than I had anticipated.

Although there are several records in the local library extolling the virtues of Nelson in general, there seem to be very few records belonging to individual firms that have survived the amalgamations and take-overs of the last decade. The Lancashire textile manufacturers were notoriously tight-lipped about what they were doing in their own mills; they were seeking to weave new and attractive fabircs to suit customer demand, and competition was keen.

The mill in which both firms were operating, when John Hindley and Vernie Haighton set off on their travels in 1927, and in which

Hindley Bros. remained for the next thirty years was called Bankfield. There is also reference in the diary to silk being woven at Fold Mill, this was a newly-aquired mill and was situated at Bolton.

Bankfield Mill was built in 1895 as a cotton mill, and at the turn of the century was weaving calico. The mill, which was well-built of stone and several storeys high, is little changed in outward appearance to this day. In the early part of this century single-storey weaving sheds were built with their roofs mainly of glass, or 'north lights' as they were called. These sheds were near or adjacent to the mills, and there was plenty of space in Nelson—as compard with some older mill towns built in narrow valleys. The operators of the sheds in this part of Nelson changed as demand of various firms fluctuated, but by 1927 Hindley Bros. were running looms in Vulcan and Eagle sheds as well as at Bankfield.

Built near to the Manchester-Colne road, and being close to the railway, Bankfield Mill is reasonably well situated; coal and yarn would come from futher west in Lancashire. By this time, however, the Leeds-Liverpool Canal, with its magnificent climb over the Pennines, was being superseded by improved rail and road transport, for although the canal runs through Nelson on its way from Burnley to Barrowford, few early 20th century mills are to be found beside the canal in this area.

It is interesting to reflect how this particular part of Lancashire grew during father's early life. Nelson was not an old town, but it was near to the old towns of Colne and Burnley and to the village of Barrowford, transport was convenient, Nelson Corporation was go-ahead, and there was plenty of space on which to build.

Every schoolgirl knows—especially if brought up in these parts—about the evolution of the textile trade; of the cottage industry of cloth being spun and woven from the fleeces of sheep roaming the local hills, to the growth of large industrial complexes—the 'Dark Satanic Mills'—in the valleys; here it was in reality.

The high moorland traits on the boundary between Yorkshire and Lancashire have traditionally been an area for sheep farming; for hundreds of years cloth has been made from the wool of the local hardy sheep in the upland cottages. There was an abundant supply of water for cleaning the fleeces, it flowed in rivulets and streams from Trawden Fell and from the majestic Pendle Hill which dominates the area. The damp climate was ideal for keeping the spun yarn in the right condition.

As methods improved and water power took over from hand-spinning and weaving, so mills sprang up near more vigorous supplies of running water further down in the valleys, such a village was Barrowford and as the area prospered, an attractive residential area grew up the hill towards Blacko.

It was at "Moorlands", Blacko that John Hindley was living in the year that he set off on his travels. He was at the home of his eldest brother Harold and wife Gertrude, and their only son Reg who was fourteen at the time, and to whom John writes warm and friendly letters—as if to a younger brother.

In those days many members of the family lived within the area and convenient by a short walk and a tram ride to the family business in Nelson, but now the younger relatives have dispersed as the traditions of a textile family have died, and most of the people of my father's generation have passed away.

*   *   *

John Hindley's father hailed from Manchester, he was the sales director of the firm of Barlow and Jones, merchants of fine cotton. This firm was still going strong in 1927, as the agent in South Africa, a Mr. Muir, seems to have really gone out of his way to help, and possibly to impress, young John Hindley when he was out there; perhaps the Barlow and Jones agent was a bit too busy entertaining the two Englishmen, as he does not appear to have had much time to help Vernie or John businesswise.

Although John Hindley, senior, was very sucessful as a cotton merchant, his two elder sons, Harold and Arthur, turned at quite an early age to manufacturing and to setting up on their own. How much they were encouraged towards this end by their father, and whether he foresaw the demise of the cotton industry and that the future lay in developing new fabrics, is hard to say. However, the choice of district both geographically and commercially was wise. The sons would have had the advantages of a ready market, in the early days with their goods through Barlow and Jones; they would also be assured of prompt payment for their cloth at a time when many merchant would be slow to pay.

Thus the eldest Hindley brother, Harold, went to Nelson to a local mill to learn the trade, (Arthur's career was somewhat interrupted by the First World War) but soon the two elder brothers had set up at Bankfield Mill, Nelson under the "room and power" system.

Working the "room and power" was a system prevalent in the

factories at this time; it became a means whereby a man with only a little capital, but with plenty of ambition could start up on his own. The renting of "rooms and power" sprang up as a way of getting round the Governments' Company Law of the 1900s, large amounts of money were being made by the cotton trade at the time and owners were building large factories which were in danger of leading to over-production. With this new system the owner and the manufacturer were not the same person. A "room and power" company would build a mill, provide power and steam, and let off parts of the mill to firms who wished to become manufacturers.

We have evidence of this system at Bankfield Mill in the early days by two instances: one was a sale catalogue in 1903 of the sale of the contents of that part of Bankfield Mill rented from the Bankfield Room and Power Company by a cotton manufacturer who was to cease trading, included in the sale were 600 looms for weaving calico: the second instance is the report of a fire in *Nelson Leader* in May 1914 which reads "The most disastrous fire in the history of Nelson broke out last night at about 11.00 p.m. at Bankfield Mill, Nelson. The mill, owned by the Bankfield Room and Power Company, contained about 1,200 looms which were run by the two firms, Messrs Hindley Bros. and V. E. Haighton and Co. Damage estimated at between £30,000 to £40,000 was caused and 700 workers were rendered idle . . . The flames could be seen from miles around, and an estimated crowd of 12,000 had come from neighbouring Colne and Burnley to watch the fire . . . Hindley Bros., manufacturers of satin cloth, had only recently installed a large amount of new machinery." One result of this fire was that the firm formed its own force called the Tacklers Brigade, they practiced regularly and earned themselves high tribute two years later with their bravery in the fire of the neighbouring mill.

This disastrous occurrence at Hindley Bros. however, would not have concerned young John Hindley much at the time, as he was only eight years old: it is interesting, however, towards following the fortunes of the business, as the firm is no longer referred to as making mainly cotton, and satin cloth was the forerunner of the weaving of artificial silk for dress fabrics. At the time they were actually using a cotton warp and an artificial weft to make strong but shiny mattress-cover cloth.

We do not know exactly, when between 1903 and 1914, that the family started up in Bankfield, but we can ascertain from contemporary accounts why they were attracted to the area; the facilities were there and there was still room for expansion. Soon after the mill had been built a contemporary writer relates to the growth of the town.

"Three miles north of Burnley is the town of Nelson, a steam tram takes you there and you travel along the Colne Road. Nelson is conspicuous for the rapidity of its growth, and perhaps no town of its degree in Lancashire has made such progress. You may look in vain on older maps for it . . . Named after Lord Nelson when the local inn-keeper was fired with enthusiasm over the victory at Trafalgar, he named his hostelry at the four-lane ends the Nelson Inn. The little group of houses round it gradually became identified with the name, but it was not until 1844 that the town was officially recognised.

"In ten years the population has doubled, the wondrous growth has been the subject of admiring comment in the Cottonopolis into which its fabrics have found their way in increasing quantities . . . There was one mill sixty years ago, now there are sixty mills with a total of 33,000 looms."

By 1908 Nelson was engaged in the manufacture of worsteds, silk and fancy dress goods. From the outset the mills had been weaving fine cloth and so the looms and expertise were readily adapted to modern trends: the Nelson weavers were renowned for their skill and any work seen to be badly done was referred to as "Burnley woven".

Nelson Corporation were actively promoting the area by the year 1927, and the Nelson Textile Society produced a journal, so we have a fairly good idea of how things were at this time.

The room and power system was on the decline, firms were able to buy their premises, and the corporation was responsible for producing electricity and there was a new generating station for the provision of lighting and traction (I presume that this means trams). There is a strange comment of the electricity committee getting benefit from the burning of the town's refuse. The tramway was extended from Barrowford to Higherford—which is adjacent to Blacko. Letter-post was delivered four times per day, which was an important asset before the days of universal telecommunication.

There is also mention of Nelson making Fancies whereas Burnley was making plain bleached cotton cloth and drills for export to India, China and Far East. There is mention in the diary of some of the cloths which were principally made in Nelson at the time—voiles, poplins and sateens, and the problems of weaving stripes and checks in

"Bankfield Mill" Nelson Lancashire.

the coloured goods trade: but more interesting is the frequent mention of artificial silk.

In those days all the talk was about art silk (later referred to as rayon). Certainly Harold Hindley was one of the first of the traditional cotton manufacturers to put his faith in this new-fangled—and as some people thought, preposterous—idea of making cloth to be made into garments out of wood-pulp (viscose) and later out of chemicals. No wonder these textile men were reserved about what they were doing.

★   ★   ★

Having understood a little of the commerical and business world about which John Hindley writes, it is interesting to consider how his upbringing would affect the style and tenor of his writing. The impression is of a rather solitary young man; happier in the company of older people and with adult conversation. It is not until several weeks of the voyage have elapsed that he seems to relax in the company of those who are his own age. I can well rememeber his great love of nature and knowledge of the countryside, also an affectionate and critical eye for horses. Certainly he seemed a man who might have been happier in a different walk of life, and yet he was totally involved in the textile environment.

Sadly, John Hindley, senior, and his wife died when father was an infant, he was brought up for a time by his elder sister May—who was married to Vernie Haighton, and then lived during his teens and as a young man with his elder brother Harold. He went to boarding-school, but it was certainly not in the family tradition to aim for university; and specialist training, in engineering for instance, would have been considered inappropriate. He would have gone to technical classes as there was a good college in Nelson or Evening Institues as they were called. In those days a young man would go through all the processes of the mill; setting-up the looms, winding, weaving, and maintaining the machinery, and with "early starts", before graduating to visits to the Manchester Cotton Exchange. It was surprising that John mentions in his diary in India that he had never before seen the whole process of cotton preparation; this was done further west in Lancashire and nearer to Liverpool.

I am reminded of the dry sense of humour which my father had, and which is so common in Lancashire. He said that as a young man he was always trying to make his early start before Myers, the mill manager who was a real tyrant; one dark winters morning he really thought that he had managed to get to work first, only to be told by the boilerman that it was barely four a.m!

There was a certain feel about the textile trade which I can remember as a child, and which lasted well into the middle of this century. Not only were one's uncles and cousins in the trade, but also most of one's friends. The ancillary trades, loom-makers, foundries, printers and dyers were all round about. Although there was a very marked distinction between the workmen and women, and the management, everyone knew everyone else, as they had all been born and brought up in the same area. There were no whizz-kid managers in those days: it was the working of the machinery, and also the weavers and their families which were my father's main concern—today it would have been classified as the job of the technical adviser and personnel officer. For good or ill, this close-knit communtiy has gone forever.

To some extent however, even for the boss and his immediate family, it was an insulated life; some of the remarks in the diary would today be considered naive such as John's very fleeting remarks on the General Strike. He was to return from his world-wide travels to troubled times. In Nelson there were serious strikes by the tacklers and weavers. Employers attempted to hold down wages and introduce modern machinery—and the Depression of the 1930s lay ahead.

In order to set the scene as to how things really were when my father set off on his travels, I set out to write to many people who would have known my father in the late 1920s; perhaps I left it twenty years too late, as so many family and friends who would have had an interesting tale to tell, have passed on: this industrial history is of no interest to firms which are vast complexes and which took over most of the family textile businesses. Recently, quite by chance, I learned that the chairman of our local District Council had been a weaver at Hindley Brothers in 1928, and I asked him for his recollections. I also received a letter from the last mill manager.

When one is aware of the sort of conditions at home John Hindley is comparing with such topics as the printing of cloth, labour in the Indian mills, and the early self-service canteens in Sydney, then the remarks of the diary become much more relevant.

The final part of this background includes memories of a weaver and a manger and extracts from four of the most interesting letters which I received from people with first-hand knowledge of the 1927-28 period.

* * *

"Recollections of learning to weave when I left school at the age of fourteen in 1928."

Tommy Cardus—Craven District Council
15/8/84

Hindley Bros. of Nelson had mills on Bradley Hall Road. There were three weaving sheds—one at Bankfield Mill, and two nearby called Vulcan and Eagle sheds.

I started work in Eagle shed and was put with an experienced weaver called Fanny Eastham to teach me the trade. At that time a full complement of looms to a trained weaver was four, but a learner weaver graduated to four after learning on two looms only.

At that time the looms were plain single-shuttle ones, and we were weaving fine cotton cloth. The weaver was responsible for bringing her own weft yarn from the weft-cellar to her loom, and for carrying her own pieces of woven cloth to the warehouse, also for cleaning the four looms: this resulted in reducing running efficiency of the looms because they would be stopped and standing idle whilst the weaver carried out these unskilled ancillary duties.

Hindley Bros. had the foresight to introduce ancillary labour to relieve the weaver of these unskilled duties; and this, along with fitting both warp and weft stop-motions, increased the running efficiency of the looms also improved the quality of the woven cloth.

At a later date, larger shuttles and an increased size in the weft yarn package, resulted in the weaver being able to work more looms than the standard number of four.

In about 1930, Hindley Bros. changed over from weaving cotton cloths to weaving art silk fabrics—later known as rayon fabrics—using viscose. About this time, all the old Lancashire calico looms in Eagle shed were scrapped, they were replaced by six-shuttle circular box looms from Billy White of Colne—loom-makers. This type of loom being able to weave six colours weft-way and any number of colours warp-way, and with the addition of a dobby to the loom we were able to weave different pattern motives in the cloth.

Conditions in a weaving mill at the time that I became a weaver were hard, but one had pride in a job well done.

There was no canteen to have your meals in: if it was too far for you to go home in your dinner hour you took your own food, you brewed your own mug of tea from the steam-heater water boiler, and then ate your meal sat on a stool at your looms. A labourer was in charge of brewing up the boiler, and it was his duty—amongst other things—to keep the boiler clean inside and out.

I remember a story about a weaver who accused this man of having a dirty boiler because her tea tasted funny, he took offence and to prove his point brewed his own tea but had to agree that it did taste queer. Whilst they were pondering the cause of this funny taste to the tea, along came a young man from the warehouse, lifted the lid of the boiler and took out four black-puddings which he had hung in a muslin bag in the boiler in order to warm them up.

My early recollections of Myers Hartly, who was mill manger when I first started there, were of a large-built man, feared but respected and with a droll cynical sense of humour. He always wore his bowler hat when walking round the mill. He was without any doubt the man who motivated the sucess of Hindley Bros. Two incidents stand out in my memory regarding the man.

When I was learning to be a loom overlooker, or tackler as they were called, we had to provide our own tools. As I was then on a very low wage I had bought my tools for the trade from a second-hand shop, and what a motley assortment these tools were. One day as I was working at my bench, Myers Hartley noticed my tools, and asked me how I managed to carry on my work with such an odd assortment. I told him that it was all I could afford. The following week he brought me a full set of hand-forged spanners made by the blacksmith at Hindley Bros. other mill; I told him that I could not afford to buy them, so we agreed that I should pay sixpence out of my wage until they were paid for. As the weeks went by no sixpences were deducted from my wages: the next time I saw Myers I mentioned that they had not started to deduct sixpence per week for my spanners. "What tools? What sixpences? I know nothing about it," was his reply I was never charged for those spanners.

The other incident was at the time of year when a local firm of builders had been called in to whitewash the roof windows ready for the summer months, but the work had to be carried out without stopping any looms. I was stood at my work-bench as there were no weavers waiting for my help. Myers came over to talk to me, he stood watching them for a short while and then said to me. "I will now show you how to put a workman in his place regarding the work he is doing." He banged on the steam pipes with my hammer to attract the attention of the foreman (they had put planks across the overhead steam-pipes to stand on whilst they whitewashed the windows with a Turk's head brush mounted on a pole), when the formean who had been beckoned and had climbed all the way down, Myers said to him, "When you have finished whitewashing the floor, you can start to put some on the windows." When I looked on the floor all I could see was two spots of whitewash about the size of a half-crown.

After Myers Hartley, the next mill manager was Jim Ashworth, more often called Jim Ash, he was another Lancashire character, and worked hard with success for Hindley Bros.

I can see him now in my mind's eye, stood at the mill gates at 7.00 a.m. starting time, watch in hand wearing a black alpaca jacket, his spectacles on the end of his nose. Straight up seven o'clock he would lock the mill gates, and anyone late for work might as well go home. At that time any weaver absent from work, whatever the reason had his or her looms given to what was known as a sick weaver; these were unemployed weavers who were looking for work, they ran the looms until the weaver on sick absence returned to work; the sick weavers always at the mill well before starting time.

When Jim Ash died, Hindley Bros., on the day of the funeral, closed the mills for the day without loss of pay to the work people.

★   ★   ★

(Letter from Cunliffe to V. Cutter 20/8/84)

Cunliffe worked for the firm of Hindley Bros. for fifty years, he started as a weaver and retired as a manager. As well as remembering these early years, he was to see the fluctuating fortunes of the firm in subsequent years.

Nelson 20/8/84

Dear Mrs. Cutter,

Many thanks for your letter of the 30th July 1984.

It certainly reminded me of my early years with the firm of Hindley Bros., at Bankfield Mill. In fact I commenced working for the firm in 1924 and continued until my retirement in 1974.

I started as a weaver, and then cloth inspector in the mill, later I was overlooker, then shed foreman and manger. During this time I had connections with the brothers Harold, Arthur and John, but it was mostly with John, as he was about my age.

I remember John coming into the mill to learn to weave. He was put with a teacher weaver who had six looms. I had only three looms (beams to him) in the next alley, and consequently saw much of John's progress—or otherwise! I remember he put two shuttles in the loom (that is, he forgot to take the spent shuttle out when changing it and started up the loom) and causing a smash and breaking a large number of ends out. His punishment to take up★ most of the ends that were down. There was a saying in the old days. "That you never made a weaver until you had put two shuttles in!" So after that episode, John considered himself a weaver.

During this time we wove cotton sateens, twills and poplins, and satin stripe shirtings some with coloured stripes; also a few corset cloths which were a heavier cloth with an artificial silk warp.

Your father also spent some time in the various sections of the mill to gain experience such as the preparation departments, design

★ It would mean rethreading hundreds of loose ends.

departments and on the sales side also. All this, of course, happened before th world trip that you mention in your letter.

I remember your father's return from his world trip quite well, because it was after he returned, when changes began to take place in the mill. He certainly came back with modern ideas of running the business.

In early thirties we branched out into weaving ray-de-chines and crepe-de-chines, using an artificial silk weft. This proved a difficult period owing to the handling of the yarn; which was so very lively, that it caused many problems. But, eventually these were overcome, and very soon being handled as well as ordinary cotton.

As the quality of yarn and warps were improved, and the handling of the same, it became obvious that more looms could be run per weaver.

Mr. John was a great advocate of the more looms system, and it was introduced under great opposition from the weavers' union. After a period of dissention, soon the weavers were working six, and eight looms, and later twelve looms each.

During the Second World War we were switched over to government work, which meant weaving cloths for the Army and Air Force. Cloths for uniforms, overalls, etc. We also wove specialized nylon cloth for

John Hindley on his hunter "Gypsy" at Paythorne.

parachutes. All these cloths were subject to government inspection which was of a very high standard.

After the war we continued to develop the nylon trade, making fabrics for underwear, dresses shirtings, etc. for such firms as Marks and Spencers.

A period I clearly remember was the overlookers strike at the mill in about 1938, when all the union men were sacked and the firm decided to train their own men. During this time the brothers, particularly John, came quite regularly in the evenings to help out, and worked with the foreman and the managers of that time.

Another thing I remember about Harold and John was that most Saturday mornings they would walk round the mill in either plus-fours and sports jacket, or riding gear, johdpurs, etc., according to what sport they were taking part in on that particular day. Of course mills used to work on Saturday mornings until 11.00 a.m. in those days.

On most days during the week Mr. John would walk round the mill, and anything that he saw that displeased him was recorded and a note would be on my desk for my attention.

You will be aware of subsequent progress after the merger with Samuel Holden, then Carrington Dewhurst, Vyella, etc.

These are just some rambling memories as I have thought of them, but I hope that you may be able to glean something from them which may be of help to you about those early days.

Yours,
James Cunliffe.

*   *   *

(From a letter to V. Cutter from Madge Mayall 29/3/84)

Madge was the youngest daughter of Samuel Holden, a cotton manufacturer near Nelson. She was close in age to John Hindley and her elder sister Beatrice married John's elder brother, Arthur Hindley.

Upton-upon-Severn.
27/3/84

Dear Val,

Thank you for your letter which I received this morning. Your queries made me think back a long way. I really knew very little of the Hindleys until World War I when they moved to the large red bungalow in Blacko, we, of course, lived a few doors down at "Mount Pleasant".

When the senior Hindleys died Harold, who was by then married to Gertrude Haighton, had previously made the old three-storied house at Fence Gate a home for Arthur, Dora and John.

Your father was at school at Mill Hill when he, Harold and Gertrude came to Blacko, whilst I was at a French school in Sunningdale, occasionally we would travel to London and back together. We were both very much the youngest in our families, and we were lonely. We liked walking and bird's-nesting, and had a rota of nests to visit each week in the Easter holidays.

Harold was a very astute business man, intensely keen. Arthur was an officer in the Royal Artillery, and was quite badly injured when his horse fell into a crater. At the end of World War I Arthur went straight back into the business.

I remember that Harold was always very kind to me, as he was with all the members of the family who were subordinate, but he was king pin. We always felt that as he grew up, your father was not given the responsibility he should have had by Harold. Giving his younger brother horses and expensive gifts does not really pay for a heritage lost.

Your father went on his world trip with Vernie Haighton because it was convenient; Vernie was going, and was willing for John to go with him for your father to gain some experience. The whole trade was sinking into a depression at the time which lasted well into the 1930s. It was very bad when I was married in 1931. As you say, it was customary for all cotton manufacturers to be very tight-lipped about any innovations in the fabrics, and about what they were doing.

I was very fortunate in my early memories of Holdens Mill. We all knew and were familiar with each piece of machinery and had to inspect anything new that was bought. I must have spent hundreds of hours in the mill, helping the weavers and winders, or just gazing at the endless wheels whirling around—and finding a use for them in my mind's eye.

We were taken to the loom makers, cotton spinning firms, to the fabric finishers and to the Manchester warehouses.

I probably had a more general knowledge of cotton than your father had at that time. I do not remember your father having much special training; I think he went through the mill with early starts, I remember him telling me about boiling a kettle to thaw his car out in the early winter mornings.

Your father said that he almost put his had on a small green snake which was deadly, whilst he was in India—that detail of his trip has stuck in my mind.

From our teenage days we were always friends.

Madge.

*   *   *

(From a letter to V. Cutter from Audrey Catford 9/11/83)

Audrey was the daughter of Doctor Catford who was both the consultant to Harold's wife, and a close family friend.

Quidhampton, Nr. Salisbury.
9/11/83

Dear Val,

How sad it is though, that once the older generation is no longer there, so many questions that they could have answered remain.

I know that my father started in Torquay in 1923, so that if he met Harold and Gertrude as early as 1927-28, they must have been among the early friends he met through attending the Imperial Hotel, where I know they stayed on many regular occasions.

Captain 'Jack' Hance on his brown gelding "Ecstasy".

As so often happened with my father's outgoing personality, they clicked and became firm friends. I remember that Gertrude seem to suffer from some permanent malaise, and that Harold was always so touchingly solicitous for her.

Certainly my parents met Reg during that time when he was a very young man. Even at that time, or subsequently, he had a real flair for horses, and my parents marvelled at the way he could pick up quality horses on his trips to Ireland and then train them as show hunters. I remember staying at the Royal Pump Room Hotel with them during the Bath Horse Show and getting Hance's autograph—but that is only a fleeting childhood memory.

I fear that is really all I can remember of your family in the early days. With best wishes

Audrey.

(From a letter to V. Cutter from Lee Cornes 31/10/84)

The Cornes family were also cotton manufactuers in Nelson at this time. Lee's uncle was married to John Hindley's sister, Dora.

Stoke-on-Trent.
31/10/84

Dear Val,

I don't think there is much we can tell you about Nelson and the textile trade in the 1920s except that it was a difficult time for us all once the post-war boom had exploded. Credit was hard to get, and most of the manufacturers were at the mercy of their bank managers. I seem to remember being told that the only reason several of the larger firms survived was that their banks could not afford to let them go.

I think Cornes and Co. were in the process of changing from cotton to synthetics like so many other firms, and times were hard—particularly for the weavers who would find their looms given to a stranger if they were only a few minutes late for work whatever the reason might be. Good luck with your project.

Yours Lee.

★　★　★

(Letter from the late Albert Aspinall to V. Cutter 28/12/83)

Albert Aspinall was an importer of textile machinery. His letter forms an important link as it tells of what happened after John's world trip. He was a close friend of John Hindley, and became my godfather in 1935.

Lytham St. Annes.
28/12/83

Dear Val,

It has taken a little time (for an old man of 80 plus) to assemble his thoughts for the details you call for in your letter.

My understanding of the early days was, that in the late 1800s Mr. Harold and Mr. Arthur moved to Nelson from their merchanting activities in Manchester. They set up a weaving business in Nelson where they took rooms.

The textile industry was in a reasonably healthy state in 1927, and it was in this year that I joined a Manchester firm whose object in life was to import and install modern textile machinery from Europe, and later from America.

It was from this move that I first made the aquaintance of your father.

In the early 30's, after my chief had died I took over as pedlar. It was from this move that I first got to know of your father at Bankfield Mill. Like all locals mills—or most in Nelson—they were pioneering the weaving of art silk on non-automatic looms which had been built locally. Whites of Colne was one loom maker, others were made in Burnley.

I took the Crompton and Knowles agency in 1936 and began to peddle automatic looms, but it was 1945 before I broke the ice at Bankfield.

That year—or was it 1946—the British Rayon Weavers' Association (of Manchester) was encouraged by the government to send a team to the U.S.A. to learn the developments of the American textile industry that had been made during the war, and to study their methods of production. The team included your father, Johnnie Duckworth, Stanley Emmott (of Cowling) and a male secretary; the team was lead by Mr. Joe Nelson*.

I was invited by Crompton and Knowles to be available at their

*Eldest son of James Nelson.

works at Worcester (Massachusetts) to meet the team, and was subsequently seconded to them for a grand tour of the mills, especially those in the south, i.e. in Carolina.

Your father and I by that time were good friends. I had already had the good luck to introduce a modern method of winding (Swiss Schweiters) which had helped to increase the number of looms per weaver.

After our tour—all went out by sea and back, as no air travel was available then—Hindleys decided to try out the Crompton and Knowles S6 automatic loom. A small order for 24 was placed and the looms ultimately installed at Bankfield.

Nelson at that time was known as Little Moscow, there was no, or very little, co-operation from the tacklers or weavers during the trials.

This resistance proved too much for Hindley Bros. who decided to build a mill at Horton Bank Top—a suburb of Bradford. The City of Bradford co-operated by building new houses for the mill operatives. We installed some automatic looms, and the trials, in spite of some oppostion in operation, were a success.

The looms were delivered and installed during 1947-48-49. The Marshall-Aid Plan, which was set up directly after the war by the U.S.A government gave assistance with extremely good credit terms between the nations involved (not individuals). As far as I was concerned, the looms were rationed and sold on a quota delivery basis. In one way this was a good thing, because the change-over to automatic weaving at the mill was thus a gradual process—but to me it was lousy because I had to wait so long for our commission!

Finally—your question about world trade in the period I have written about. All I can say is that it was a near boom period for the textile industry; and your family business was one of the leading successes in their particular field during this time. But now, alas, what a sad change to an almost impotent industry as far as Lancashire is concerned. How many mills are there in Nelson today? Blackburn had 120 mills when I was a young man, today it has two.

Yours,
Albert.

INTRODUCTION

Lancashire to South Africa

LIVERPOOL — TENERIFE — CAPE TOWN — MUSSENBERG — BAIN'S KLOOF — KIMBERLEY — JOHANNESBURG — PRETORIA — DURBAN — KIMBERLEY — CAPE TOWN.

V. Cutter
10/4/84

★ ★ ★

The sea voyage to Cape Town from England took three weeks, with a brief stop at Tenerife. Tourism had already come to Tenerife a century before in a moderate way, it was an important resting and trading post for the early colonists sailing south for South Africa and Australia. Many wealthy colonial families would spend the winter here: there was also a strong British influence through the wine trade. The fine old capital city of Santa Cruz being described as "busy with commerce and shipping".

Cape Town and the surrounding countryside make a tremendous impression, as does the visit to a Dutch farm and the car journey over the picturesque mountain pass of Bain's Kloof. John Hindley's remarks about the size of farms and the attitude of the Dutch farmers could have been made one hundred years before—a comment on the farming habits of the Boers in 1830 goes "They are accustomed to large grants of land which is in abundance; the colonists are few and they seldom cultivate more than for their land and their cattle. Instead of a moderate size farm he must have the district for himself . . ." The government restrictions in the 1920s tended to discourage permanent improvements to farms and there was a growth of isolated farms and homesteads.

Much of the railway system in 1927 would have been comparatively new, as, following the discovery of diamonds in Kimberley and of gold near Johannesburg in the previous seventy years, there had been a tremendous boom in railway construction for the necessary movement of people, freight, and coal: but by the early 1930s the gold mines were already showing signs of exhaustion, and the depression had started.

Durban had been growing very fast in the sixty years previous to John Hindley's visit. During those years the marshes and reef had been dredged in order to open up the harbour, the vast hinterland had led to an enormous amount of traffic by sea, and the town was being popularised as a seaside resort.

Some of the most interesting parts of the diary are where John Hindley gives an account of conversations with fellow travellers—train journeys appear to be much more conducive to intelligent dialogue than do sea voyages. There is a conversation with a South African cattle dealer with his opinion of the immigration prospects, and also of the Australians: another account is of the problems of farm droughts and credit systems.

John Hindley draws his own conclusions in his last letter from Cape Town about the textile trade and agencies; and the prospects for South Africa generally.

OUTWARD BOUND

Tuesday   *21st June, 1927*
We left the Princess landing stage, Liverpool, at 4.00 p.m. on board the S.S. *Desmosthenes* bound for Cape Town. The Mersey was quite choppy and rain threatened at about 4.45 p.m. but it blew over. The pilot left us about 8.30 p.m. off the north coast of Anglesey, and we were abreast of Holyhead by 9.45 p.m.

I am very impressed by the number of coastguard stations off the Welsh Coast, I never imagined that there were so many.

I find that there is a Mrs. Store on board, and that she is bound for Cape Town. The mother of the "Burton Bank"* Stores' family is a Mrs. F. E. Store and they also come from South Africa. The rest of the passengers on the list do not look very interesting, but I hope some of them will be.

Have heard that South Africa on the whole is not a very good

---

* "Burton Bank" is a house at Mill Hill School.

place for the wireless on account of atmospherics, and interruption by shipping; also that there is a lack of good programmes, and that the outdoor life detracts much from its popularity.

My legs ache very much owing to the motion of the ship, it is 10.30 p.m. and I have decided to turn in. The weather has improved and the wind freshened, but the ship is very steady. It is still light and I have put my clock back eighty-five minutes. Suggested amounts for tipping are—deck steward, head waiter, cabin steward—ten shillings each; money is deposited with the purser at 1%.

244 MILES

Wednesday

I have enjoyed today very much and the time has not dragged at all. I have played quoits and deck-tennis; I might find that I enjoy the other games better, but these could have been worse; deck-tennis is quite strenuous if played properly.

There are two hours rest time between two and four p.m. during which no games are allowed. I worked at some Pelmanism for most of this time and quite by accident found a quotation from Aristotle which is very applicable to myself. "We all know of men who would be transformed if they only knew what to do with themselves when at work."

I like the passengers better now and find that some of them are quite interesting; most people appear to be colonials returning home from leave, or going out to new jobs; some people are going out on business, but no one seems to be going on a trip like myself.

At night a few of us danced for a short while.

550 MILES

Thursday

Nothing of any special interest happened this morning although we did see a number of fishing-boats and a few steamers. At night we passed Finistere; the ship is still wonderfully steady and we have had a following wind all day, from noon yesterday until noon today we have sailed 326 miles. I played a few games of croquet, quoits and deck-tennis, the tennis was very strenuous. A sports' committee been elected.

I had quite a long talk with "Carmelita" or Constance Talmadge, otherwise known as the girl with the red hair and the even redder lips. She is a film fan and rather fancies herself but she is quite amusing.

Miss Martin seems a nice sort of girl and quite good looking, in fact in a black evening dress she can give points to anyone on board; she also dances very nicely—not like the little stiff ones.

I have learnt nothing about the trade today worth recording. As far as I can judge, although people talk about South African cotton, no one seems to know much about it.

The old lady at our table is Mrs. Winder, sister-in-law of William Winder of Winder McKlean, the cotton merchants. She is seventy-two and is travelling alone, she is always up early for breakfast and is wonderfully active.

Saturday

Saw my first flying fish today; they are very pretty but much smaller than I had thought them to be, I expect them to be larger further south. They are very like large mackerel with two pairs of fins which are used as wings, as soon as these wings dry the fish drops back into the water. Their flight may last one hundred and fifty yards but fifty yards is more the usual distance, occasionally they fly on to the deck of the ship but normally they just skim the top of the water.

TENERIFE

Sunday   *26th June*

Fourteen hours ahead of time.

I sighted Tenerife at 2.05 p.m., the atmosphere was very hazy and we were within five miles of land before we saw the cliffs. We were fortunate in being able to see the peak which, being 12,000 ft, is perpetually above the snow-line.

From the distance the island looked like one bare rock devoid of vegetation and inhabitants, as we drew near we were able to distinguish beautiful white-looking villages nestling in the steep-sided valleys, and also to see crops growing in terraces on the mountain-side.

On arriving in the harbour we were boarded by the pilot who took us to our anchorage, it was four o'clock by the time we were anchored in Santa Cruz—which is Spanish. Immediately swarms of natives came on board wanting to sell us lace, beads, baskets, bad cigars and all sorts of things that we did not want; also they came to pick up anything they could lay their hands on. They are not above entering any cabins which have been left open, and fishing for your things with boat-hooks through the portholes.

Santa Cruz de Tenerife, Plaza 25 de Julio, La Fuente.

With these robbers came many rowing boats with divers who dive for silver—copper being indistinguishable in the water; there were some very good performers, and one diver had only one leg. I got a photo of his dive from start to finish; I hope this and my other photos come out all right.

We had to pay 1/6d to go ashore in a launch, the distance was only about half a mile. The ship's lifeboats are not used on such occasions. I suppose the natives must be allowed to make a living where they can.

On shore we met more "robbers" but we were not tempted to buy any cheap cigars. Five of us, including the Bishop of Pretoria, went to see the cathedral and the museum. Much to my disgust Brown took Miss Billie Martin with him, the more I see of him with her the more I dislike him. We hired a seven-seater Buick which was in very good repair.

The town, in fact the whole island, is much more modern and up-to-date than I had imagined it would be. Practically the whole island is laid out in terraces owing to the tremendous slope of the land. The main road from Santa Cruz has a tarmac centre with tramlines on the right, there is a rough broken surface for the use of horses and pack-asses on the left-hand side. The road contains a tremendous number of hairpin bends with the occasionale half-mile straight, the car climbed very well for most of the time in top gear, but the road looked too twisty and steep for trams. The view all the way up is very fine as the land drops away so quickly and the atmosphere is usually very clear. It is a much better road than one would have thought possible when seen from the ship.

The lower part of the town was very poor-looking, narrow streets with only just enough room to pass one another. The houses were mostly three or four stories high on each side of the street, but because of the intense light—the sun being practically overhead all year round—they would not be so dark inside as they would have further north. The window space was very small and for the most part shuttered below, it appears that people use the top rooms and keep out the glare with sun-blinds. I managed to get a glimpse into the interior of one of these houses, it resembled the rooms of a workman's house in Lancashire with a large family; the same untidiness of the living-room, and similar glittering ornaments and awful pictures in the front parlour; but if I had to choose I would go back to Nelson.

The amount of motor traffic was very surprising, Ford buses by the dozen, also Buicks, G.M.Cs. and Overlands; there were also a few French and Italian cars, Renaults, Citroens, and Donnet-Zedels, Lancias and Fiats. The only English-made vehicle was the Royal Enfield motorbike and side-car. However, there were English advertisements in many places from Dunlop tyres and Sunlight Soap.

The horses and mules were in a terrible state such as would not have been tolerated in England, fortunately there did not seem to be many of them. The pack-asses were in much better condition: I suppose that they were privately owned and the owners knew the fable about "The camel and the straw". The oxen, of which there were not many to be seen, looked splendid animals, there were four working in a cornfield and they had coats like well-conditioned hunters, I expect that they were both worked and milked.

There was a great variety of goats to be seen from very small ones to some bigger than I have ever come across before, the largest of the goats looked to be about ten hands high, I could only judge their height from the man who was with them as I could not get very near; the man had very patched trousers, so perhaps they were fierce! I saw very few dogs about and most of those I saw were of doubtful parentage.

The people of the island seem to be divided into two dstinct races, the dark swarthy ones who looked to have some negro blood in them, they eat onions and try to sell you anything you do not want, and a fairer race who lived further up the hill above the meaner part of the town, these people might be taken for English or other European races and appear to be of rather better class. I was rather puzzled by this as the races who have conquered and inhabited the island have been the Spanish and the Portugese—so must try to find out a bit more about the history of the Canaries.

The children were very clean and their white clothes really were white. What a change to see clean children playing in the streets after seeing them in the smoky streets of Lancashire and Yorkshire, of course I must remember that it is during the week when I see the children of Lancashire and I am comparing them to a Sunday here: here they may look very different during the week.

The general dress of the people here is as that of the North European but adapted to the conditions and the climate, the styles are the same as those seen in England in the summer but a few years out of date. There was a little artificial silk to be seen but mostly of very low quality, what struck most was that there were no prints about, as they were just the sort of people that one would have imagined to wear gaudy ones. We saw some sort of religious procession, some men were wearing drill suits and others were wearing black, quite a number of men and boys were all in white with white taped wound lattice-wise up their legs from ankle to half-way up their calves, they nearly all wore black hats which made them look a proper load of cut-throats.

The smallholders who lived on the island appeared to be a very happy and contented lot and quite industrious, in fact I have never seen such intensive cultivation, often plots which were only a couple of feet wide would be planted with oninons and potatoes between two cornfields. There was a lot of ripe corn much of which had already been mown. There was also a luscious green plant about eight feet high and with leaves about four or five inches wide, each plant had a lovely poise, it was one of the most beautiful crops I have ever seen and when we saw some oxen eating them I longed for some myself.

The flowers that we saw were by far the most vivid, though too gaudy to be called the most beautiful, that I have ever seen; I cannot recall having seen any grass. There seems to be no proper system of drainage of water from these hills, but everywhere are to be seen deep dry channels waiting to carry the water to the streams with which the hills abound in the rainy season.

In spite of its shortcomings I was fascinated by Tenerife, and would like to stay a couple more days and study more of the people as well as the plant life; but on making enquiries about the island amongst the passengers most of them failed to see its attraction and were glad to get away from it.

TOWARDS AFRICA

Wednesday   *29th June*

Nothing very thrilling has happened during the last few days. I have got knocked out of all the competitions for which I have entered and, apart from letting my partner down, I am rather glad. It is getting much hotter: pleasantly hot when doing nothing; damned hot when playing hard. I have started to eat less, in fact I do not enjoy my meals except for the fruit. I still have a cough which hurts when I have an empty stomach, I cannot account for it except that I smoke too much.

Yesterday and today we have seen dozens of dolphins or porpoise and a great many flying fish, I have just seen the fin of a shark. I have always been too late to photograph the dolphins, I doubt that my photos of the flying fish will show up on the screen at home. Today we also passed through a lot of very interesting species of jellyfish, they are known as the Blue Bottle or Portugese Man-of-War, they are about six inches long, pink in colour, and so constructed that part of them looks like, and actually performs the duty of a sail.

We passed through a few rain squalls just as we were off Cape Verde, I was almost tempted to put on my swimming costume and go out on to the deck, as the rain looked and sounded so deliciously cool. We had quite a good view of the African coast it looked very picturesque with palm-trees growing along the water's edge, this is the last time we shall see land until we are near the Cape.

Tuesday   *5th July*

We are now about three hundred miles south of Ascension Island, we have not seen any land for nearly a week; in fact all we have seen is a few ships and those passed us at night.

Wednesday   *6th July*

It is rather difficult to remember if anything has happened during the last week or at least anything worth recording. It is getting fearfully hot and people are beginning to tire of each other.

Thursday   *7th July*

Oh, what an aimless sort of life this is, to get up and have a stroll before breakfast or not, according to how we feel; play games, read, or do nothing at all; eat, play or not, eat some more, and in the evening we get some exercise by a little dancing. I realise more and more the enormous truth in the fact that man is never so happy as when he is working. My trouble is—how shall I work? I do not appear to possess the necessary amount of drive, if for a time, I had to work in order to eat, it would do me the world of good. I wonder where I shall be in a few years time if I do not pull myself together, at present I am not the slightest use to Hindley Bros., and that state of affairs must cease.

I am having a very slack time of it at the moment which may pay in the end, as my cough does not get much better and it does it no good getting hot and out of breath at the same time. That is no excuse, however, for letting my brain get addled and that is what I have been doing, not only now, but for the past few years; unconsciously perhaps, but now I fully realise it; and the curse of it is that it does not worry me as it should. As I look at the passenger list I cannot find anyone in a similar position to myself, anyone else with the start in life that I have had would have got ahead by now.

I wonder if I could settle in the colonies and if so what I should do there. I am again faced with one glaring fact, I have never made a success of anything either at work or play, at school-days or since; riding I enjoy immensely, but do I take enough interest in it to get to the bottom of it and learn how to ride really properly? *No!* I am keen for a few days or perhaps weeks and then when getting down to brass tacks I come across a problem and my interest flags, only to be revived again at the same spot later.

The same applies to motoring, I get a lot of pleasure out of it, and often imagine I should enjoy tinkering about with the car but when half-way through a job I get tired and do not finish it as well as I started it. With everything I can think of it is the same, tennis or photography, and worst of all—the same applies to my work.

THREE DAYS FROM THE CAPE

Friday   *8th July*

Another day nearer port, I do not know whether I shall be sorry or glad to leave the ship; in some ways I shall be sorry as there are a few nice people remaining on board but I think that the odds are in favour of disembarking at the Cape. It is just as well perhaps, as I am getting to like Billie better every day, and as I have nothing else to occupy my time—at least nothing of importance—it is inclined to make me moody.

I have not made myself popular with a lot of the passengers, those of about thirty and over, who try to be ten years younger, make me very tired.

The older people I do not find nearly as easy to get on with as at home—of course, so many people knew my father, or knew of him—and that makes a tremendous difference. Whilst not openly resenting my intrusion into their conversation, I feel that the older people are not too thrilled about it, they do not think that anyone of my age ought to have an opinion about anything. I am still lapsing into my old habit of not first considering what I am going to say and choosing my words carefully before opening my mouth, so far I have not made a fool of myself but some day I shall come an awful cropper if I am not careful; it is not how it sounds to me that matters but the effect on the company present.

The younger people I get on with quite well, rather an unusual thing for me as I do not generally hit it off with people of my own age: on board it is different as people do not behave as they normally do on land. It is a great pity that we English as a race do not mix more freely, I hear that the colonies have no use for formality. I wonder which is the lesser of two evils? I should imagine ours to be—I shall be interested soon to find out.

I wonder how old Billie is? Anything from twenty to twenty-five. Sometimes I think she is very young but she is so sure of herself without being cocksure and objectional about it: I cannot help thinking that she is at least twenty-four, if so I certainly by rights ought to have had the cold shoulder by now, but she is hardly the sort who would do that: she has by far the nicest disposition of anyone on board, if all the New Zealanders are like her I must certainly try and go there. But it is time I stopped this—I shall probably never see her again after I have got off at Cape Town, if so I shall have very pleasant memories of one of the nicest girls I have ever met and I shall never be disillusioned.

Today I have seen my first whale, we have already seen a few spouting in the distance but this one we nearly ran down, it broke the surface not fifty yards from the ship. We also saw a school of porpoise in the distance but I was unable to photograph them.

Midnight

The ship is starting to roll a bit, having been very steady. It has been a gorgeous day, cooler than the last few days but with beautiful sun, sky and sunset.

Saturday

It is afternoon and the roll which started last night has now increased and it is enough to slide the chairs about in the lounge and the library, it does not seem to have upset as many people as I expected. It is not easy to walk but not so bad if you keep your knees slack.

Midnight

I am just about to turn in after quite an interesting time of it. Richards, one of the boys from the third class, spent the evening with Miss Sheffield, Miss Dunlop and myself at the picture show, he seemed to be a nice sort of fellow and I should imagine that he would get on in life through hard work. We afterwards had our fortunes told by Miss Dunlop. Richards said that his was correct as far as it went, I could find nothing correct about mine.

The swell continues much to most people's annoyance, I do not mind as it give one more room to move about and it keeps the decks clear. I have had a long day being on deck since 7.15 a.m. and have been walking about most of the time. It is a good job that I am leaving the ship on Monday as another three weeks of the company remaining on board would be rather upsetting—ambiguously so—for me.

Sunday

The last day on board, and I feel sorry now that I am leaving I have really had a very good time, but I suppose it is to my own advantage to leave now.

About two o'clock we sighted a very large cargo ship but I could not make out her line. I first sighted land about three o'clock and after that we never lost sight of it. We had a very beautiful sunset at about five o'clock and just after that Table Mountain—complete with a cloud known as "the table cloth"—came into view.

Shortly after dinner we dropped anchor in the bay and everyone went out on deck to see what they could see. The cloud had lifted and I think that Table Mountain in the moonlight was the most impressive sight that I have ever seen, with the lifting of the clouds we also had a wonderful view of the mountains. Cape Town with all the lights glowing looked very fascinating, and the sight made me hopeful of the morrow.

We had a bit of a sing-song after dinner but I soon got fed up, I walked and talked with Gwen Kenrick for quite some time, then paced the deck by myself for about an hour, later Mrs. Mackintosh joined me until about midnight when she turned in. Having nothing better to do I also turned in about half an hour later, but really felt that I could have gone on walking around for hours if I had anyone interesting to talk to such as Miss Kendrick or Miss M., but not having anyone I was as well in bed.

CAPE TOWN

Monday   *11th July*
Probably the most eventful day of my life, if I were to return home tomorrow I should not consider my trip had been a waste of time.

I was called at 5.30 a.m. and managed to get on deck some time before six. I had a good look around the bay, saw what there was to be seen in the misty half-light and then, making sure that the sun was not intending to rise for some time, I retired to my cabin to complete my packing. Breakfast was at eight and then the imigration officer came on board: everything was straightforward for me so my next visit was to the customs officer who had also come aboard. I declared everything and had to pay £5 duty on my camera and field-glasses—to be refunded when I leave if it is within less than six months—I also left all my films, but later discovered that I could have taken the unexposed ones into the country. I found the customs officer awfully decent and helpful in advising me what to do.

About ten o'clock, after saying goodbye to various people, we went ashore with Freeland who got us through customs without having a bag opened. He then took us round the town to look at various hotels, and also out to Sea Point which looked very nice, but we decided to stay at The Royal as it is so much more central.

After arranging about our rooms we went to Freeland's office to discuss business and then out to coffee. I was interested to hear him talk of the youths out here: those who have been brought up in South Africa and have been waited on hand and foot since childhood, have no idea of discipline, and will not get down to rock-bottom in their work: they get responsible positions without ever having been first put in their

places—namely at public school. Of course, I must remember that this
was being said by someone who was not himself brought up in South
Africa.

We spent the afternoon in the park and went to the museum. It was
very intersting to see the spring, summer and autumn flowers which we
have in England, all blooming at the same time: snowdrops, narcissi,
gladioli, montbretia and various other home flowers amongst
subtropical bushes and trees: most of these had very little foliage and
some none at all, they looked very pretty from a distance but lost their
charm when viewed too closely on account of the vivid red colouring
and lack of leaves.

The museum was very interesting but like all museums it contained
too much. It was only possible to take in a little at a time so I spent my
time in the rooms containing animals and fishes. The white rhinoceros
was one of the biggest surprises that I have ever had, shaped like any
other rhino but as big as a medium-size elephant. The giraffe is also
bigger than I had expected. In the skelton room there were some
complete skeletons of whales which were colossal, the jaw-bone of one
was fifteen feet long.

At night we went for a run with Freeland in the car, the scenery was
very beautiful in the moonlight and everything looked so big—but it is
always difficult to judge size and distance at night. I do wish we had
been travelling in an open car and then we would have felt the full
benefit of it. The roads are very twisty and although the hills we met
were not steep it needed a car with a good engine to get over them on
account of the sharp corners. Oh, for the Lagonda! I would soon show
them what a 12 horse-power car could do on these hills if the gear-box
was used properly.

The road surface was much better than I expected, in fact, in some
parts, especially near Cape Town, the road was splendid. The coast
road round Hout Bay and on to Chapman Point is a superb feat of
engineering, being completely cut out of the sloping face of the cliff.
The coast is very wild and grand, it has a most majestic appearance
when compared to other rugged coastlines that I have seen; it is
probably more impressive when seen at night than during the day, but I
shall not forget it.

We arrived back at about 11.30 p.m. and I got to bed about an hour
later, I was ready for it having been up for nineteen hours and having
walked more than I have done for weeks. The Royal Hotel where we are

staying is nothing to swank about, being rather a cold-looking place, but clean, the food is excellent and the attention is amazing.

I feel unable to describe Cape Town as I have not yet had time to form an opinion. The traffice moves at a terrific rate, especially on corners, there are gullies in the roads so the cars go fast to avoid touching the bottom when passing over them. The weather is wonderful, they call it winter but I could manage quite comfortably with a shirt and blazer this afternoon. At night it grows cold but it is a nice sharp cold without an icy wind or anything unpleasant.

Freeland has promised to take us to a Dutch farm and to Rhodes' house, he has also arranged to take us up Table Mountain—I am very keen on the latter.

Tuesday   *12th July*

Had breakfast and went for a stroll in the town, although we were able to see some of the ships from where we were it seemed that the *S.S. Demosthenes* had probably already sailed. We then went back to the hotel and I wrote for a bit whilst Vernie went to see Freeman, I decided to walk down to the docks hoping against hope that the *Demosthenes* was still there—of course she had gone and I felt very fed up that I had not been able to see Billie again, also I had arrived at the wrong side of the dock. The only big ship in was the *Windsor Castle*, and it took me an extra half-hour to get back round. I arrived back at the hotel just about done in having been away for about two hours, the exercise had been more strenuous than I have been accustomed to for the past few weeks and I was beginning to feel the heat.

Have just read some interesting paragraphs in *The Argus*. "Bad trade at present is attributed to the drought: also to unrest over the Flag Bill*." "Someone proposes building three-roomed houses for £150 each." I suppose this for the Cape Coloureds and it is strongly opposed in the paper.

---

* "Flag Bill" in 1927 the final design for the National Flag of the UNIA was decided, the Union Jack having only a small central position.

The Royal Hotel,
Cape Town.
12th July, 1927

Dear /

I have such a lot to write about that I don't know however I shall finish before the mail leaves on Friday.

We had a very good trip and were very happy on board, now that the ship has gone I feel quite lonely. It is rather an aimless sort of life on a ship, it is impossible to do anything properly as there is always something to disturb you: if you settle down to read someone sights a whale or wants you to join in a game.

Tenerife I found to be a most interesting place—of course, never having been to a foreign place before it would be more interesting to me than to most people. The only town of any importance, and the only one we saw was Santa Cruz, it was for the most part a poverty-stricken place. There were some fairly wealthy people on the island but not many. On Sunday the men seem to favour wearing black hats, they look bad enough, but a dark skin under a black hat looks awful.

From Cape Verde to just north of Cape Town we never saw any land, at one time we were four and a half days without even seeing a steamer. About 36-40 hours before reaching port here there was a very heavy swell, striking us almost broadside on, and the ship had a tremendous roll.

We have had beautiful weather since we arrived in South Africa, beautiful to us that is, some places only a few hundred miles from here have not had rain for two years and consequently the cattle have died and left the farmers penniless.

I don't know what to think of Cape Town, it reminds me of Dublin and yet it is as different as possible from it, the only word to describe it it "unfinished". It has some wonderful buildings but they are rather spoilt by odd ones that do not come up to standard. In some places the English and Dutch architecture clash badly in style.

Will write further about conditions and the state of trade when I have been here a few more days.

I suppose Fold Mill will be running all right now. I hope that there is plenty of work to keep it going, and that you are getting better deliveries of silk.

Yours,
John.

Table Mountain, Cape Town.

Post Card to—Master Reginald Hindley,
'Moorlands',
Blacko,
Nr. Nelson, Lancs., England.

Dear Reg,

I have not much news since last time. I have not sent off the rhino hide as I cannot pack it properly but have sent several other things, the hunting shield, etc. You can open any of the parcels addressed to myself.

If you want anything special from Australia do write immediately, then I can look round a bit. I hope you are having a good summer hols.

Love from
John.

Wednesday   *13th July*

This diary is becoming quite a curse, what with writing letters during the day and this at night, I seem to do nothing but scribble.

Whilst V. was working, I took a bus to Sea Point and then walked to Camps Bay, returning by train. The walk was rather further than I had intended but I enjoyed it immensely.

I am beginning to like the residential area better now as a visitor but I would not like to live there, the coast is certainly beautiful but I think I would prefer to live out in the country. The houses look very well set in the hillside, their cream and white tones stand out against the dark background of Table Mountain, nearly all the houses are plaster-faced—in fact all that is required here to build is some third-rate bricks and plenty of good plaster. I notice that quite a lot of the houses have their garages on the roof, this is because the houses are built into the hillside and the road runs above them and the only place to gain access with the car is driving on to the roof. Some of the gardens are very pretty, the flowers look much better now that I am getting use to them and the creepers on many of the houses are really delightful.

During the afternoon Vernie and I paid a visit to J. Nunnery & Co., the wholesalers, they did not seem to be very interested in any of the samples we had to show them, and apart from a silk check on a voile background I saw very little of our class of cloth, the main line, as elsewhere, seems to be heavy khaki drill of about 8oz. for shirting, we also saw some very heavy blue-printed drill which would be heavy enough for trousers, the trouser cloth was even more coarse. Nunnery's did, however, let us look round, I was surprised that with the exception of native lines large wholesale stocks are not carried, apparently they only stock one dress length each of many different patterns, the shop-keeper will only buy 3½ yard pieces of each length—the reason being that a white woman does not want to get a frock only to find that very soon a native woman is to be seen in the same thing.

We afterwards went through a shirt factory run by two Jews who didn't look as thought they had a cent between them. It was quite an interesting place but the quality was coarse, they seemed a couple of cut-throats. The factory was only small, having a production of 400 dozen shirts per week, but the owners had already made £40,000 to £50,000 out of it.

Thursday   *14th July*
I spent the morning looking round the poorer part of the town, the

native areas are not as bad as I expected but I did not see the worst district. I also had a look at some of the industrial area; there seems to be quite a lot going on at Salt River, the flour mill is a wonderful place, there is also a big ironworks which I think belongs to Baldwin's. On the way back from the docks I saw one of the most beautiful sights I have ever seen or ever expect to see; the left point at the edge of Table Mountain had a rainbow right across it, the sight was so wonderful that it is no use trying to describe the colours—I defy anyone to do so—I never imagined that there could be such gorgeous ones.

In the afternoon I finished my mail and lazed about a bit. We set off at about four o'clock for the Dutch farm at Constantia Neck⋆ to dine with the Boulers. Freeland had some calls to make and it was almost dark when we arrived, the mountains looked really beautiful in the sunset, the colours on the pinnacles and in the valleys varied from gold to blue, purple, brown and almost black; there is no doubt that the country is growing on me hourly.

We had a very nice meal, perhaps too much, but otherwise splendid; I never thought it possible to be so absolutely at home in a stranger's house—and what is more remarkable is that they are Dutch—before I left I felt that I might have known them for months, and I am quite sure it would have been necessary to have known an English family for several months before getting on such good terms.

We left at about nine o'clock as Freeland had to go to fetch someone from Robertson, which is about 130 miles away, and I went with him. Fortunately for Freeland, though unfortunate for me, we met about half-way up Bainns Kloof. In spite of not going right over the pass I got a fair idea of the vastness of the country. The mountains looked lovely in the moonlight but sometimes we drove for eight or ten miles without even seeing a farmhouse. The roads were really terrible and several times I touched the roof, the "slats" or water gullies are sometimes over a foot deep, and they don't half give the car a shaking. On the way back I dozed off a little, the greatest compliment, and incidentally an accidental one, that I could have paid Freeland as a driver—he is a madman with a car. It was about 1.30 p.m. when we got back. I was disappointed at not going over the Pass and I must try to see it in daylight before I leave Cape Town.

⋆ "Constantia" is the name given to several old wine farms outside Cape Town. "Neck" is the South African word for a narrow ridge of land adjoining two mountains.

City Hall, The Parade, Cape Town.

Friday   *15th July*
    I still do not really know what to think of Cape Town, it is an old
town and there has been some difficulty in modernizing it. The
Standard Bank, Parliamentary Building and the Post Office are by far
the finest buildings. The Post Office is really enormous considering
that the population is only 130,000, but it seems to be kept very busy.
The white population is 70,000 and most of them are in some sort of
business and the fact that Cape Town is an important seaport would
increase the volume of mail enormously.
    I spent the morning at the docks watching a ship berth. I had hoped
to find Dr. Eric on board but as it had sailed from Liverpool Eric was
not there—he is probably on the *Medon* which I am told does not call
here. If she does not call at Cape Town where does she get her coal
from? Perhaps it is Durban.
    In the afternoon, after reading a bit and scanning the motor, I went
with Vernie to the golf links, the view was wonderful, I doubt if a better
setting for a golf course is possible.

Saturday   *16th July*
Vernie and I went to Muizenberg by train, Muizenberg is a quite
pleasant holiday resort facing the Indian Ocean and is famous for its
surf-bathing and wonderfully sandy beaches. Unfortunately it is not the
bathing season, I was surprised how cold it was as it is only a few miles
from Cape Town.

At night Freeland and Mrs. Vautt had dinner with us and afterwards
we went to see *First Year*, it was a very good show indeed. Mrs. Vautt
had to go after the first act but the rest of us went on to Markham's for
coffee which I enjoyed nearly as much as the show: it is rather an
interesting cafe with a splendid band.

The Royal Hotel,
Cape Town.
15th July, 1927

Dear /

As promised I am writing further about my impressions of Cape
Town and the general state of affairs. My views of Cape Town have
undergone a complete change during the last day, the place grows on
me and I think I could settle down here quite comfortably. The
surrounding country is wonderful, and provided I had a car to get away
at the week-end I could be quite happy here.

We go to Durban on Monday and pass through Kimberley and
Bloemfontein but do not break our journey there. After Durban we go
to Johannesburg, it takes forty-six hours by the mail train—I shall not
mind the 6.23 to Manchester after a journey like that.

People say that Durban is the finest city in South Africa, that Cape
Town is on the decline, and that Johannesburg is too much of a city of
gamblers to be of use for business—but Vernie seems to want to go, and,
of course, I do. One of the boys from school is up at Jo'burg and he is
related to some quite "big noise", so with a bit of luck we shall see
something of the mines.

It seems impossible that there is not a store of any importance
between here and Bloemfontein which is 700 miles away. Just think of
it! Twice as far as from home to Torquay and not a place worth calling
at to do business.

There seems to be very little silk about, I have seen some art silk satin
stripes on cotton pyjamas but little else of our type of goods. A person
on board took a fancy to my dressing-gown, and said she had paid 7/6d

for a similar cloth in Durban. All goods are very expensive in South Africa; food, drink, fares amusements, etc. are all 50% above prices at home.

I have been to a couple of wholesalers, and round a shirt factory run by two Jews, the wholesalers only carry small amounts of the better type of cloth. There seems to be no demand for our class of goods, the lines in which big business is done are in coarse khaki drill and native trousering.

I have learned quite a lot about South Africa and her people, Freeland has been most interesting and we had a long talk this evening with his friend, Maud Vautt. We went out to Milnerton, it was a beautiful night and the lights of Cape Town on the return journey looked very wonderful. Nothing here seems to be done in a hurry, even in business and they are very slow in legal matters.

A lot of the old farms are very extensive, some being 70,000 acres or more, although often very little of this land is cultivated, perhaps only a few thousand acres. The Dutch farmer seems to resent splitting up his land—other than the small plot of land which the Kaffirs are often given to live on. In most cases the Dutch farms have been in the family for generations and the farmer will neither sell his land or cultivate more of it, but does just enough to get a fair return for his labour.

Trade seems to be built up on a long term of credit, ninety to one hundred and twenty days being quite usual; if the farmer has a difficult season he will often sell the crop before it is ripe in order to buy seed, etc. to carry on with, as the buyer of the crop is often the local storekeeper as well, he has the farmer in his hand—as the farmer is always owing him money. The storekeeper is in a better position, because if the wholesaler will not give him sufficient credit he can always go elsewhere for it, as most wholesalers are willing to finance a storekeeper with a steady business but only limited capital.

I have not yet decided which way I am coming home but I will probably go to the Far East after Australia and then see as much as I can of India. I would certainly like to go to New Zealand, even if it gives me less time in the East. I had always imagined New Zealand to be about half a day's sail from Australia but it is about four days, and I have heard that there is a tremendous amount to see when there. Everyone whom I have spoken to on the boat said that it is the nicest country that they have ever been to, very like England and with the advantage of a good climate, and that it would be a shame to miss it.

Tomorrow we are going up into the country for a couple of days and arriving back on Sunday night. On Monday we go to Durban on the 10.30 train so we shall be fairly busy. I don't think I have any more news now, which is just as well, as I seem to have done a tremendous amount of writing since I left home.

Are you getting any better deliveries of silk yet? I suppose you will not be getting anything like the quantity it is possible to use at Fold Mill. My shirts of all silk are greatly improved after washing and are very nice to wear, of course, they don't cool very well when you get really hot, but the cotton ones are not much better in that respect in this climate.

Will close now,

Yours John

Sunday   *17th July*

Freeman took us for a wonderful run to Bain's Kloof. The country was rather flat as far as Wellington and not very interesting. The climate of Wellington is hot but very healthy, and I was surprised at the amount of industry such as fruit-drying factories, jam-making and flour-milling, there are also leather works and a waggon-making industry, as well as the traditional wine trade together with brandy and vinegar-making.

After leaving Wellington as we travelled up the pass the scenery was really wonderful: I wish I could do justice to it with my pen, but it is hopeless. The lower slopes of the mountain are quite thickly wooded with a type of fir amongst the other trees, I did not expect to find firs in this part of the world, I should have thought it was too hot for them.

We then ascended Bain's Kloof Pass which was constructed in 1854 by convict labour. The pass rises to about 2,000 ft and it is possible to see over the plain for forty miles. At one point we saw the peaks of the mountains which we were told were 115 miles away. The air is wonderfully clear.

After a lunch of chops cooked over a wood fire we drove through Wand Paarl where there are extensive wine farms; it was the original Huguenot settlement. Dutch is the language spoken here. We then went to Stellenbosch and stopped for tea before returning to Cape Town.

CAPE TOWN TO KIMBERLEY

Monday   *18th July*

Left Cape Town at 10.45 by train for Jo'burg, we had a good view of the elegant Dutch houses in the suburbs of Paarl and of the fruit and vine cultivation around Wellington. The railway runs through the Hex River Valley after leaving Worcester, and here the country is rugged in the extreme and one feels quite shut in by the mountains towering above; most of these, however, are anywhere from five to twenty miles away but as they are as high as 8,000ft and the air is so clear they appear to be much nearer.

We then got to the part of the country where the drought has been terribly severe. There is nothing but a sandy plain covered with withered and stunted bushes only two or three feet high with the occasional bush ten to fifteen feet high. For miles there is nothing and then perhaps a farm to be seen but with not a neighbour nearer than fifteen miles. Occasional small flocks of sheep or herds of goats are to be seen scavenging but how they live is a mystery; most of the animals that

The Outspan, typical Boers.

have not died have been moved to areas that are not in such a dreadful state, but it is not easy to move animals in this country.

The railway line is simply wonderful, the gauge is only 3ft 6in and it hardly seems possible that the train can stick on the lines. On some of the bends it is possible to see the first and last carriages and some of the gradients are as steep as 1 in 4·5. The mail train averages thirty-five miles per hour from Kimberley to Jo'burg, this does not sound very fast but the train has to climb most of the way, Jo'burg being on a plateau 6,000ft above sea level.

KIMBERLEY

Kimberley I did not like, there were three things that struck me most forcibly—De Beers, de diamonds, and de dust, especially when the wind blew. It must be a terrible place in the windy season as the sand and dust seem to get everywhere, nor is there much shelter from the sun. There are a few good-class buildings and one or two streets are quite fine, but the city generally seems to be decaying.

Tuesday   *18th July*

In the morning we took a tram to a small oasis which they called The Park. It was about seven miles from Kimberley, the local people seemed to think it was quite nice—so we will leave it at that.

We went to the diamond mines in the afternoon. The diamond fields cover an enormous expanse and are surrounded by a high barricade surmounted by a wire entanglement, through this wire a high tension electric current is passed. There is not very much to see, and owing to the short time available we did not take any photos. We did however, manage to see about £7,000 worth of diamonds in the laboratory.

The pulsator separates the diamonds from the ore; it is rather ingenious, working on the sieve principle until the final process, then the small stones and shale drop on to an inclined plane which is greased and has a constant stream of water running over it—the diamonds stick to the grease and the stones roll off.

It seems strange that convict labour should be employed in the diamond mines, however, care is taken that they cannot possibly escape. So that they cannot, when the time comes for their release, take stones away which they may have swallowed, they are kept for several days in a special compound and dosed liberally with castor oil. Kimberley is practically run by De Beers, they have under their control such things as electricity supply and tramways.

We went to have tea with Mrs. Store—of whom I wrote on the first day of my diary, but we had very little time there as we had to rush off for our train for Johannesburg.

JOHANNESBURG

Wednesday   *20th July*

The countryside looked pretty hopeless from the train as we left Kimberley, the same miserable outlook with dried and stunted vegetation everywhere, we were not sorry when the light failed and we could no longer see it.

If I remember rightly it must have been about 6.00 a.m. when we entered Johannesburg station and the day was just dawning. With the rather dirty air of the mining part and the train's steam there was plenty of smoke about. It was like entering a large English industrial town and I felt quite at home.

As soon as it was light the place assumed a very different aspect. The buildings are very fine and the broad streets set them off so well, the big open-fronted concrete or stone buildings certainly impress the traveller. There is no doubt that in spite of its newness—some would call it vulgarity—Johannesburg has a certain majesty. The only objection that I can make is that in the laying out of the town the streets are dead straight, and they nearly all look a like as they cross at right angles.

The growth of the town has been remarkable, less than fifty years ago it was the merest hamlet—if one can use that word (as my idea of a hamlet exists in England and England alone). Today the population including the suburbs is 300,000 and the rateable value is £5,000,000. One of the reasons for all the wonderful buildings in South Africa is that there is a considerable income tax rebate allowed for building. This low tax has its drawback however, as the exports will not balance the budget, so that everything that is imported is subject to a very considerable amount of duty. Not just a protectionist duty but a revenue producing duty, for instance, petrol in Jo'burg is 3/- per gallon.

We did not manage to see round a gold mine, I was rather disappointed but we just do not have time to see everything. Some of the mines are worked to a tremendous depth, in one of them the pit-head gear is 3,000ft below the surface and this works the cages down to another 4,000ft.

The mine dumps where the crushed ore is deposited are enormous. They are very hideous, but what can they do with the ore except build it up on the surface. The crushed ore is almost white, and the dumps give one the impression of snow-covered hills when viewed from a distance.

At night Sandy Store came to dinner and we went to a show. It was splendid to meet someone so far from our old school and to talk over old times again. I am off to Pretoria tomorrow for the day so we arranged to meet when I return to Jo'burg.

> Post card to—Master Reg Hindley,
> "Moorlands".
> 20th July, 1927

Dear Reg,

We arrived at Jo'burg at 6.00 a.m. today and I rather like it. We stopped at Kimberley for a few hours and I saw some of the diamond mines. The day after tomorrow we go to Durban.

I have met a boy from school. I have not seen any ox-gangs like this picture yet, but I have see a team of twenty donkeys.

> Love from,
> John.

PRETORIA

We caught the 8.05 train and after an interesting journey arrived at Pretoria, which is now the political capital, at 9.15 a.m. The railway line drops steadily down to Pretoria which is forty-five miles north and over 1,000ft lower than Jo'burg. It passes through the "Reef" which is the popular name for the Witwaters goldfields, I was surprised by the size and number of the goldfields, for a few miles we passed gigantic pit-head gears and were there overshadowed by dumps rising three or four times higher.

We got a good view of the native compounds, they were really terrible, without having actually seen them it is impossible for anyone to imagine the appalling conditions under which the natives live, or rather, exist.

A lot of the countryside was very bare, but not so depressing as from Kimberley. Pretoria is a much more extensive place than I had imagined it to be. It is laid out in a similar manner to Jo'burg, the streets if anything were straight for an even longer distance, one was quite seven miles long without a bend.

The Union Buildings are most impressive, they are standing on a splendid position overlooking the town from a distance of about four miles; it is one of the most impressive pieces of architecture that I have ever seen, simple and modern but at the same time beautiful, the surrounding grounds are immaculately kept—we got several photos that should turn out all right. The whole town gives you a kind of homely feeling on account of its age and historic associations.

The houses in the residential area stand in large well-kept gardens some distance from the roads, their layout gives the impression that they are much more numerous than they actually are.

We had coffee out in an open cafe and caught the 1.10 p.m. back to Jo'burg. The return journey was rather slow owing to the steep incline. After a late cold lunch I went to try and find Mr. Muir, who is representative out here for Barlow and Jones, he was not in the office so I went and made enquiries next door and found that Muir had gone to Durban.

I had quite an interesting talk to this man in the next door office, he was called Lyn Johnson and is Vyella's representative. I wish I had a bit more time and a few more introductions in Jo'burg as it is possible to learn a tremendous amount about South Africa from these people if they are willing to talk—and most of them are. They all seem very willing to talk to a complete stranger, and there is none of this "get out of my office if you have finished" attitude about them.

At night Sandy came again for dinner and afterwards we went to a show; we seemed to have such a lot to talk about I could not remember half of it.

Post card to—Mrs. H. Hindley,
"Moorlands".
22nd July, 1927

Dear Gertrude,

I am having a topping time, 5,000ft above sea-level, probably the highest that I shall ever get.

We are getting used to travelling about now, having had about three days of it in the train, and have about eight more to come.

Love from,
John.

JOHANNESBURG

Friday   *22nd July*

The following morning we went to see Mr. Nellist and he took us to the Rand Club. It is a most elaborate and exclusive place with about £50 entrance and about £20 yearly subscription. Strange to say that in a town of this size they have managed to exclude Jews from membership.

Mr. Nellist then showed us several interesting streets where rioting had taken place some years ago. I wish I had been able to spend more time with him, he could have been useful in getting us into the mines as he has access to a lot of them.

Johannesburg is a town in which many people are unable to live on account of the altitued, it affects heart cases and often noses and ears. I notice that my shaving is more difficult here on account of the quick drying of the lather. It is possible to see for great distances owing to the rarified atmosphere. During the war soldiers from Jo'burg lost all sense of distance when fighting in the lowlands of France.

We only had time for a few words with Mrs. Store, whom we met in the hotel, as we were due to leave on the 2.15 p.m. train. I would certainly try to stay at the Langham's Hotel again.

JOHANNESBURG TO DURBAN

Friday   *22nd July*

Luckily we had managed to get a compartment to ourselves. After an hour or so the countryside became more undulating with the occasional clump of trees, by exercise of a little imagination it was possible to see some resemblance to Exmoor. Although there was very little variation in the landscape there was a little more life about. Sheep and goats were in small herds, and round the odd farmstead—where the vegetation was greener, no doubt because of the small streams or springs—cattle, horses and donkeys could be seen. As far as I could see there were no substantial farms, mostly of doubtful-looking buildings around the farmstead, and further away a collection of Kaffir huts, often with their own plot of land. In the outlying areas of the farms the number of sheep and goats would not average one per acre.

Saturday   *23rd July*

When we woke up this morning we found ourselves in very different country, it was much more green and homelike. The countryside was broken without being rugged, or the vastness of the country around the

Cape. The slopes were often well wooded and the grass, although brown in some places, was a better colour, and there were the occasional green shrubs as well as evergreens.

The water supply does not seem so scarce here and the farm and countryside in general had a much more cheerful look; a big difference from the Karoo*. There are quite a number of huts and houses to be seen along the line, although the huts did not bear close inspection, they looked quite picturesque from a distance. The farms appear to be quite well looked after and quite a lot of ground is under cultivation but I did not see any good grazing land. The only trees that I can name are the banana and the paw-paw, there is also a species of red-hot poker which grows on trees and is very striking.

DURBAN

We arrived at Durban about 10.30 p.m. and just managed to get into the Royal Hotel; later however, we met Mr. Muir, and as he is well-known here he managed to get us fixed up more comfortably. I like the Royal immensely, it stands facing a large square in the centre of the city, in the front there is a large stoep which is fairly high giving a good view of the road. The bedrooms are plain but big and many of them open on to a large courtyard. The dining-room is quite good and as we are sitting at Mr. Muir's table we should get pretty good attention, it is also pleasantly lofty and airy.

In the afternoon Mr. Muir was going with a party to the races, and offered to arrange for Vernie and I to go as well: we did not want to break up his party so we went to the sea front to watch the bathers with their surf-boards, the bathing area is protected by a shark-proof grill.

After dinner we went to a show. Mr. Muir seems a very nice sort of a fellow, he has done everything he possibly could for us and we look like being very comfortable during our short stay here.

Sunday   *24th July*

Most of the morning was spent writing: this writing business gets a little bit trying but I suppose it does me good; even if my writing does not improve my knowledge must on account of having to recall what I have done and seen.

We went for a stroll before lunch. Durban is very fascinating, the

---

* Karoo. The innermost tablelands in South Africa, barren except in the rainy season.

streets are wide and the gardens and borders well laid out. Although the buildings do not compare with Jo'burg for size the town has a kinder look altogether. It is a great holiday resort—a sort of Blackpool of South Africa—but not crowded like Blackpool; the fact that you may be faced with a forty-eight hour journey to get here keeps many people away and there are few places of importance within a twenty hour journey.

Vernie and Muir played golf in the afternoon and I went round with them. The Country Club at Durban is a ripping place, the clubhouse is a model in every way of what a clubhouse should be; a fine cafe with dance floor; outdoor cafe, smoke-room and any amount of changing-rooms and bathrooms; there are at least a dozen tennis courts; and a covered car park for at least sixty cars each place being accessible. The course itself is a very sporting one, it is almost like a garden with many trees and beautiful flowering shrubs. The fairway is hilly and tricky in parts, but the background could not be compared to that of the Weinberg course at Cape Town.

Monday   *25th July*

In the morning we strolled around the shops and I bought a few odds and ends. We then took a tram to the Berea, as the residential part is called, and this I found most attractive. Most of the homes were bungalows and the architecture, though vastly different from ours, had a definite character about it. I have never seen such wonderful gardens: the flowers of all colours, sizes and shapes, intermingled with such profusion that it was impossible, whilst riding in the tram or walking, to distinguish one sort from another.

We went by motor in the afternoon to Sania, the country was quite nice and it was well wooded; parts of it resembled, in contour if not in vegetation, places round home. The roads were pretty bad compared to English by-roads, but the car was not too uncomfortable. At night we went down to the beach and I won three boxes of chocolates at the fair, more than I have ever won before at one sitting, we managed to get two children to take them away.

The Royal Hotel, Durban.
25/7/27

Dear /

I believe I finished at Kimberley in my last letter so I will carry on from there.

We have been in Durban a couple of days now and quite like it. The town has not the same dignity that Jo'burg has but the residential quarter is nicer, mostly on account of the climate which is milder and permits the growing of a great many more varieties of winter flowers.

The country was pretty hopeless when we left Kimberley on Tuesday night but it was quite a different story when we looked out of the train on Wednesday. The growth of Johannesburg has been remarkable, less than fifty years ago it was practically nothing.

We spent one day in Pretoria, going by train. The town was bigger than I thought with some very impressive public buildings.

We saw something of the diamond mines and the goldfields are very extensive. The country around here at Durban is a little more like home. The train journey was interesting, but the distances are vast, I will have travelled over 1,000 miles by train since leaving Cape Town a week ago.

26/7/27

I am rather fed up today, I had hoped to get a trip on a whaling ship, Muir had practically arranged it when we discovered that there was not a vessel in. As I may have to wait a week for another one, and I could not be sure how long they would be at sea, I shall have to leave it, as I cannot afford to miss the sailing of the S.S. *Nestor* for Sydney on 6th August. We are going over to the whaling station tomorrow in any case. I understand that they go whaling in parts of Australia so it is possible that I may get a couple of days on a whaler when I am there.

We are leaving Durban later tomorrow and go by train back to Cape Town via Kimberley, it will mean missing Port Elizabeth but it cannot be helped, to go there would mean spending even longer in the train with only a short time to see the town when we got there.

I must close now but will write when I get back to Cape Town where we hope to visit some wholesalers I have nothing more to write about at present.

Yours John

Tuesday   *26th July*

After finding that I had missed my chance to go on a whaler, we went down to the Kaffir market. I found it quite interesting but extremely dirty, I wish I had taken my camera. I was rather surprised that the natives did not press us to buy anything, I had expected them to be like the band of robbers at Tenerife but they did not seem to be interested in possible purchasers, in fact a number of the stalls were unattended.

In the afternoon we went to see Dawson and took him out to tea. He quite likes his work here and also likes Durban, as there are a few other people who sailed out in the *Desmosthenes* here he is not too lonely. At night V. and I went to see *Dorothy Vernon of Haddon Hall* at the pictures and thoroughly enjoyed it.

Wednesday   *27th July*

This morning, after messing about and wasting time, it was too late to go to the whaling station; we decided to go across the ferry to the slipway instead and see if there were any whales in; of course, there were none. We saw where the whales are floated on to the slipway and trucks are run underneath it, the whale is then taken by train to the station to be cut up and manufactured into various articles. Anyway, I was glad that I went as I got what I think will be some very good photos of Durban harbour from the ferry. The harbour bay is very extensive, a lot of it is very shallow and it covers almost eight square miles altogether.

I forgot to mention in the diary about the splendid rugger match

Country Club, Durban.

which we saw last Saturday between Transvaal and Natal, practically an international side with only two exceptions, the game was fast and open and the ground as hard as iron; I thoroughly enjoyed it. We returned to the hotel in a rickshaw pulled by highly-ornamented—but hardly ornamental—natives.

There are very few horses to be seen anywhere and the only well-kept ones seem to be racehorses. I have seen many teams of oxen of various sizes working, and even oxen pulling a heavy type of trap known as a Cape cart. One of the most interesting sights was a team of twenty-two donkeys pulling a load and along side them was a Sentinel steam-waggon; I got a photo of these which I hope turns out all right.

We left Durban on the 3.40 p.m. train and I am afraid that in my hurry I forgot to thank Muir adequately for what he had done for us; I must remember to do so when I get home or before that. Until nightfall we quite enjoyed our journey, it lay through a wonderfully fertile part of Natal that we had not seen on our outward journey to Durban.

After we had retired for the night, much to our annoyance an old man came into our compartment; he soon woke us up with his interesting conversation and we were sorry when we were too tired to continue talking any longer.

We casually mentioned that we were going to Australia and he shut up; after a few discreet enquiries, and finding that he would not offend us as we had no connection with that country, he opened up with the remark, "Well, I don't like to say anything bad about anybody—but the Australians! They'll give you honey but they'll sting you." He had been a cattle dealer, apparently of some importance as, after the Boer War he had been sent out by South Africa to Argentina to buy herds of cattle for restocking in this country. He has been in Africa for forty years and has great faith in the future of cattle and wool in South Africa, especially in the quality of wool if not yet in the quantity.

He gave us some interesting points concerning immigration, which for a man with capital, business ability or a good position offered boundless possibilities; but for a poor man very little. There is room for men in certain skilled trades although not in engineering. The problem lies if a white man is out of work, he cannot turn to labouring even if he were capable of it, it would never do for him to work alongside the blacks and he could not live off the wage he would receive. There are certain numbers of "poor whites", men who have lost all hope and self respect and have, in fact, turned native. Of the million white population of this country roughly ten per cent are "poor whites", and these are mostly broken gold and diamond prospectors.

Thursday   *28th July*

This day is worthy of a page to itself, I do not expect ever to forget it; if I do in later years I hope it is through having many more beautiful memories to replace it. When we got up about eight o'clock it was one of the most, possibly *the* most beautiful morning I have ever known.

The air was keen and there was quite a heavy frost on the ground, but it was not bitterly cold, even when riding on the outside; the clarity of the air was wonderful. About fifty to sixty miles away could be seen the Maluti Mountains, the contours and shades were as well defined as if they had been more like ten miles away. The higher mountains were all covered in snow and the wind felt to have come straight from them; it was as clean and as pure as the snow itself. The day did not improve—that would have been impossible—but it got very hot, if we had not been in the train we would have enjoyed it immensely. The countryside was a little more interesting than the Karoo, but not much.

We arrived at Kimberley at about 6.00 p.m., and just before we drew into the station we witnessed a sunset as weird as the sunrise had been beautiful; the clouds were very small but close together, they were leaden in colour and looked very heavy and stormy. As the sun set the clouds were lit up to a most beautiful red giving the impression that the heavens were afire—if I had ever been shown a painting of such a scene I should have considered the artist to have been mad.

The Royal Hotel,
Cape Town.
5th August, 1927

Dear /

We are getting near the end of our stay in this country, and sail at 3.00 p.m. tomorrow and then do not leave the ship for another month until we arrive at Sydney on 3rd September. I have not written since Durban, we had an enjoyable but rather tiring journey down here and I was jolly glad to get back to Cape Town. I shall be very sorry to leave South Africa, and I have had a good time here but, although I have seen the principal towns and a good deal of the country, I have not seen all that I wished to see.

To me the country appears to have great possibilities—it is young yet and there is no telling how it will develop—but it will long be handicapped by two things, the uncertain rainfall, and the racial and political animosity between the Dutch and the British South Africans. It is hoped that the Government's protective tariffs will help to enlarge the country's own trade and industries.

The other day I was talking to a man who had not reared a lamb for three seasons; the lambs are born but have to be killed to prevent their starvation and to allow enough food to keep a few breeding ewes alive. The remarkable thing about the country is the wonderful fertility of the soil after the rain, the bare sandy plains and the withered bushes are covered with grass and flowers within a fortnight of the rain falling; it is said that it is possible to hear the earth crack as the plants force their way through the soil.

From enquiries that I have made I gather that the quality of the wool in South Africa is very good and that people expect that the country will soon become a serious rival to Australia for wool, the chief defect of the South African wool seems to be the dirt and thorns in it due to careless clipping.

Cotton can be grown quite successfully in South Africa it seems, but it is grown further north in Rhodesia. I cannot find anyone who can tell me anything about it, what the quality is like, etc.

This week we have spent quite a lot of time with the directors of J. Nunnerly and Co. and V. has played golf with them. Mr. Haigh and Mr. Arnold have come out here to see what is wrong with their South African trade. The company have some very fine property in Cape Town and Durban but the wholesale side seems to have had a very bad time during the last two or three years; Muir said they must have lost about £10,000 in business during the last year in Africa.

During a bad year when the crops fail because of the drought the store-keeper will often let the farmer have credit to keep going; after several bad years the farmer becomes heavily indebted and eventually has to give up his farm. A great many of the farms are now owned by store-keepers who are usually Jews and are hated by all, at one time the Dutch welcomed the Jews as traders but the country is now becoming littered up with them.

Out here you have a tremendous number of clothing representatives of all sorts of firms catering for a very small population. The white population of the union is only one and a half million; take away 10% poor whites, and the Dutch farmers in the back-country who can afford but do not require good clothes except for one best suit, and the fact that shirting and trousering for the native trade comes mostly from America or is made here and is fairly coarse.

It is not an easy country for an agent to work, he usually has an office in one of the big towns and sub-agents in the others, twice a year he will tour the country complete with sample room—his tour taking two to three months. Muir has been very good to us but he did not take us round the business houses that he promised to, he was busy; but we enjoyed his company and found him very interesting.

I must close now, I do not expect that I will have much more news until we reach Australia. I am getting very out of touch with England, the local papers are 60% adverts, and 20% about the drought, the rest is mainly political, pride of place being given to the controversy over the Flag Bill (I am very annoyed about it, if England protects South Africa she should have the Union Jack included). The European news in the local papers is from Geneva and is very general.

I will write in about a month.

Yours John

INTRODUCTION

Australia and New Zealand

FREMANTLE—PERTH—ADELAIDE—SYDNEY—MELBOURNE—SYDNEY.
WELLINGTON—NAPIER—WAIRAKEI—ROTORUA—AUCKLAND.
SYDNEY—BRISBANE—CAIRNS—THURSDAY ISLAND.
Trip Canberra, Melbourne, Adelaide etc.

V. Cutter
10/4/84

★ ★ ★

Most of the travelling done in Australia was by sea, as many of the major towns in Australia are ports: judging by John Hindley's account of the state of the road when he drove out from Sydney to Melbourne one day, the sea journeys would be preferable. Arrival by sea was the ideal way to witness the labour troubles at the docks. Fremantle was a relatively new industrial port; the gold rush in 1890, harbour improvements, increased farming output, and the construction of the Trans-Continental railway in 1915 had all contributed to its prosperity.

The general prosperity of Australia is reflected in the remarks about the shirt factory which he visits in Melbourne. The seat of the Federal government was in its final year at Melbourne (Canberra was still under construction), and in those days Melbourne was larger than Sydney.

Sydney was the focal point of the trip, and most of the business and the enquiries into the textile trade were done here. The total time spent in Sydney was over a month, excluding various trips and diversions. The most interesting accounts are those of the wool sales, Grace Brothers the large departmental store, with its cafeteria and supermarket, the like of which had never been seen in Lancashire; and the building of the Sydney Harbour Bridge.

Life on an Australian sheep farm and the vastness of the country are well recorded after John Hindley spent a weekend at a station a hundred miles north of Melbourne.

The trip to New Zealand seems to have been made rather on the spur of the moment, partly one judges, because of the glowing accounts of that country from fellow passengers, and partly in the hopes of seeing Billie again.

A book on New Zealand bought by John Hindley out there, shows many picturesque scenes in black and white photography with sketches and pastel drawings; the corn is in stooks in the fields, and the children go to school on horseback: the largest building in Wellington is only seven stories high, but the harbour is very full with ocean-going ships. Wellington was the capital city at that time.

Napier would have also looked very different as it was before the devastating earthquake. The present factory and airport are built on land which was then part of the seabed.

From the number of photographs which John Hindley kept of the geysers and boiling pools they seem to have impressed him a great deal, and the fishing trip at Lake Taupo was fairly typical. It seems to be the one period in the trip when he does not seek or express an opinion about the country or people. Perhaps there was not time, or New Zealand was so like home.

During his second visit to Melbourne from Sydney, John Hindley's remarks about the Labour Premier of Queensland were topical, as he was on the way to Canberra. Theodore was the member for the Commonwealth Party in 1927, in spite of charges or irregularities he rose to the treasury in 1930, and attempted radical cures for the depression, meanwhile a charge for fraud over the sale of mining shares was being brought.

On finally leaving Sydney the increasing temperature was probably more conducive to letter-writing than to sight-seeing as the S.S. *Taiping* steams north to Brisbane, Cairns and Townsville.

The comments about Thursday Island have been inserted at the end of the chapter as they lead one more towards thoughts of sailing to the Far East.

TO AUSTRALIA

Sunday   *6th August 1927*
    We left Cape Town at 3.30 p.m. on the S.S. *Nestor*. In a way we were sorry to leave as we have not seen all; I wish now that I had extended my

journey somewhat. This last week has been somewhat tiresome, perhaps because Vernie and I are seeing a little too much of one another, but we must be thankful that we do get on quite well together. The only people we knew at the landing-stage were the Beyer girls who had come to say goodbye to Miss Dunlop; it was much nicer to see someone we only knew slightly, better than being seen off by friends and relatives.

We are very pleased with the ship and expect to be very comfortable, there seems to be a younger and more boisterous crowd here than there was on the S.S. *Desmosthenes.* The people at our table are not at all bad and I think I shall be quite happy with them, unfortunately everyone knows everyone else as they have all been on board for some time, however, as their parties have split up I shall soon settle down all right.

An Australian has been telling me something of the Chinese. He has a great respect for them and regards the educated and soberminded ones as very fine men. They hate war and look down on soldiers, and are honest and hard-working. In order to prevent the Chinese working long hours in the textile factories in Australia and undercutting the whites, they have had to amend the Factory Act to include one-roomed workshops under the heading of factories.

17th August

We have been on board for nearly a week and a half, I am getting disgustingly slack. I ought to find the time to study as the other people are not very interesting to talk to and I am out of all the games and competitions. It is a splendid opportunity for getting some work done but my will does not seem to be strong enough to keep me at it when everyone else is playing. I have been doing some Pelmanism during the past few days to try to improve my knowledge and memory, but really must make an effort to get through it.

We had wonderful weather for a week until the roll started on Sunday night, it did not claim many victims and as I have thoroughly got my sea-legs I enjoyed it. Yesterday was much calmer and today, although the sea has been more broken and the wind high, there has been very little motion of the ship. At about seven this evening the wind started to freshen, it is now an hour after midnight and the weather looks quite threatening; the wind is strengthening from the west, the moon is watery, and the seaspray—which is probably ruining my dinner-jacket—is occasionally reaching the boat-deck. Tonight I am thoroughly in love with the sea: it is now so much more interesting than the flat calm that we have experienced most of the journey, and I have hopes of a storm before we reach Fremantle.

18th August

There was heavy rain at about eight o'clock this morning but the rain soon cleared and the following sea was calm again; I was sorry that the weather had not lived up to my expectations of last night.

I did a little Pelmanism and tried the effect of "I can" this afternoon, I willed myself to go to sleep for fifteen minutes—which did not take long—but instead of waking up at the time I had thought of I did not wake up until four o'clock. I will try that again tonight.

Today has not been a success, it has been as bad as most days: looking back I cannot recall a single profitable conversation during the last twenty-four hours, in fact looking over the last ten days it is difficult to recall many. I have only learned of the problems that the Australian meteorological experts have in determining the duration and intensity of storms as they cannot get good information inland and we have to rely on reports from other ships.

20th August

Our last day before reaching Fremantle, I shall be very thankful to see land and even more thankful to get ashore for a while. There are a few people leaving the ship at Fremantle—I wish there were more as I am fed up with most of them.

I never met a less talkative and more uninteresting crowd, if they do not know anything about a subject it is very difficult to get them to pay any attention, I should have expected people to try to learn something by discussion with other passengers on a long and monotonous voyage like this. Mr. Melrose is the only one to go out of his way to enquire about things that he wanted to know. I find some of the people remarkably difficult to talk to, some of course, are too refined to mix with everyone—not that we want them to, whilst others are only interested in the unimportant things of life, such as the cinema, plays, parties, and the Edgar Wallace type of novel (I could do with some myself at present). I quite like Crusty, it has taken a fortnight to get more than a few words out of her but I like her better for keeping herself to herself a bit and not angling as some of the others do, and of whom I am very tired.

T.S.S. *NESTOR*
Blue Funnel Line.
20th August, 1927

Dear Harold and Gertrude,

We arrive at Fremantle tomorrow and I have just realized that we shall be able to post letters from there. I have not started to write any letters since leaving Cape Town so had better do some today.

I have been disappointed with this part of the trip, it is very uninteresting when we sail for fourteen days without seeing land, or even sighting another ship. Everyone gets very bored with each other and we shall all be glad to see land again. There are some nice people on board, but on the whole they are not as nice as the people on the *Desmosthenes*.

I have not been able to learn much about Australia as most of the people do not seem inclined to talk—I expect they are too fed up to bother after six weeks at sea. I was surprised to learn that, between ship touching the first port in Australia and leaving the last port, the Australian government receive a duty of about fifty per cent of the value of everything sold or used on the ship itself and this includes food eaten, coal used and even paint—consequently there has been a lot of painting going on during the last week.

We have had some wonderful weather, the first week was so hot I needed only a cricket shirt. We hope to have a few days in Adelaide and Melbourne before we get to Sydney, Vernie has quite a lot of business to do in Sydney so we shall spend some time there. Galbraith has suggested that we leave the boat at Fremantle and go by train, but I do not fancy spending a week in a train going across a desert just to get to Sydney one week sooner.

The African railways were wonderful, much of the land they pass over is little better than a desert and there is also a tremendous amount of mountainous country to be traversed.

I have been thinking about taking the China route but cannot get much information, no sailing lists are to be had here and no one can tell me much. To go to Yokohama, Shanghai, Hong Kong and back via Singapore would cost £50-£60. I think it would be a mistake not to see something of the East, as it is so totally different from anything in Europe. I would not see very much except the ports as most of the time would be spent sailing, but I think the expense would be worth it. I would also like to see something of India, but it would probably mean getting a slow boat round the coast to see Calcutta and Madras.

Either way will take an extra six weeks: I have not talked it over seriously with Vernie, he does not seem inclined to discuss his homeward journey until he has seen what business there is in Australia, but we shall probably part company in Sydney after a week or so and meet up again in Ceylon for the homeward journey in early March.
Midnight.

I had better finish this letter tonight as I shall be too busy looking out for land tomorrow. We had quite a good time this evening, a few speeches badly composed and badly delivered in which a few people buttered each other up uncommon. There are about twenty passengers leaving the ship tomorrow but we do not lose the majority until we get to Melbourne.

I am longing for a good gallop, or even a good run in the car would relieve the monotony; I think I shall have a donkey-ride in Melbourne if I can find nothing better. The noise of the weaving shed would be a relief after the monotony of the noise of the ship's engines twenty-four hours a day.

We expect to arrive at Fremantle at about 5.30 p.m. tomorrow, and have time to go into Perth for the day and sail from Fremantle for Adelaide at eight on Tuesday morning; that is of course, if the dock labourers will work—which they are quite capable of refusing to do. This ship was once laid up in an Australian port for six months, with only the officers on board, owing to a strike.

I suppose by the time you get this letter the best part of the year will be over whilst here we shall be getting it very warm. We are steaming north-east tonight and it is already getting much hotter.

Reg, I suppose, is home from school now and it will seem like a full house at Moorlands. I hope you had a good time in Dublin; but perhaps you brought part of the horse-show home with you.

I must close now before I fall asleep. Actually I have found that by going to bed later, say after midnight and getting up at seven, I feel really fresh—but I should need longer if I was working all day. There is never anything to do on board after 11.00 p.m. so I usually go to my cabin and read or write until I get to the sleepy stage.

I hope you are all well and having some decent weather, it is a pity you cannot have some of ours for a few weeks.

                              Love from, John.

AUSTRALIA

August 21st

Sighted land at 2.06 p.m. I think I was the first passenger to do so, it is surprising how everyone brightened up at the sight of it. I was not in the least impressed by Fremantle from the sea but it was after dark before we drew near. Although the pilot was on board by 4.00 p.m. we had a long wait for the doctor and were not able to land until after dinner.

We went for a stroll around Fremantle and then went to the pictures which were rotten. After returning to the ship we had a quiet sing-song until 11.00 p.m. when most people retired. I thought it would be a good idea to watch the Australian stevedores at work, so after finishing a few letters I stayed up and watched them unload until about three in the morning.

The men did not come on board until midnight as their union forbids them to work between midnight on Saturday and midnight on Sunday, so the first sling of cargo did not touch the wharf until 12.40 a.m. In England it would have only taken half the time.

We grumble about the unions at home but we have none like there are here, they practically run the country. They get 12/6 for the day shift which includes an hour for lunch and 20 minutes smoke morning and afternoon—compared to 9/- per shift in England—they also get double for working at night.

Instances have been known where slings of cargo which were only a few pounds over union weight have been returned to the ship's hold after touching the wharf and had to be re-slung 200lbs lighter; no one can say anything or else all work stops immediately; on the last trip some crates and cases were left owing to trouble in one of the holds and all hands striking. All this union trouble will have to cease before Australia can develop fully. We at home are asked to buy Empire products and to lend these countries money, and then they hamper our ships in this way.

22nd August

In spite of not getting to bed until 3.00 a.m. and being up again at seven I feel as fresh as a daisy and have continued to do so although it is well after midnight. I went into Perth today with Sheffer, Bezley and the Pickering girls. We had quite a good day, Perth is a nice town, there are only 50,000 inhabitants but I was struck by the prosperity of it—by

Hay Street, showing Town Hall, Perth.

the way, there are only 300,000 people in the whole of Western Australia.

We looked round the town hurriedly, and went to the pictures and then a variety show, the first was poor and the second was rotten; at the pictures we saw a film of the Prince of Wales winning a race on Dark Corsair. We did not see much of Perth but what I saw reminded me of a mixture of African towns. There was no time to look at the shops, much as I wanted to I could not very well with the others there. I ate waffles for the first time, I also weighed myself—my weight is 10st 4lbs with my clothes on.

P.S. TO LETTER TO HAROLD AND GERTRUDE

20th August

We had a very good day ashore, as Vernie was playing golf I went to Perth with some of the others, we did not do much except to buy records and go to the pictures and the theatre; we felt in a mood for enjoying ourselves rather than sight-seeing.

I stayed up last night to watch the cargo being unloaded it will do one good to return to England and see people work after seeing the dock men here. I will tell you more about them later but at the moment I want to go ashore a bit before we sail. I have been making further enquiries about my journey to the East, and will write from Sydney when I have more information or you can if necessary cable me at The Commercial Travellers' Club in Sydney. I have just been on the *Orama* to have a look round, she is one of the Oriental Line and is very fine; but I think I shall stick to travelling on the smaller ships as the people on them are much nicer as a rule.

Must really close now as I have not much time to catch the mail. J.H.

FREMANTLE TO ADELAIDE

24th August

We are crossing the Australian Bight and are two days out from Fremantle. The weather last night was not rough but at times blustery and we rolled a bit but the Bight promises to be very tame. I did not sleep as well as usual and felt very wide-awake half the night: the wind is rising now but the sea is very calm.

I spent the evening with the Kings in the purser's office, we had a very good evening discussing all sorts of subjects; music hall artists; businessmen, the advantages of travel, equality of the sexes and women in the smoke-room; the hospitality and courtesy of various nations; hotels and the class of people who travel these days; the Anglo-American debt (King is an American); taxation and landowners, etc., etc.

ADELAIDE

24th August

We had arrived in the bay by about midnight but had to drop anchor for the night and did not berth in Adelaide until 9.00 a.m. on Sunday morning.

A party of us went for a motor run to Mount Lofty and apart from being thoroughly chilled we quite enjoyed ourselves. The contour of the country was very English, and the grass a most refreshing green, as Adelaide and the surrounding country have a very good rainfall. The gum-trees were very scrappy, just as they were in South Africa, the eucalyptus were rather better they are a bit more stately and in a way

Floating Palais de Danse, Adelaide.

they remind me of oak trees. One of the most pleasant experiences of the trip was to see and smell the mimosa—or wattle as it is called in Australia: there are about twenty-five varieties of it here from fine feathery-branched ones to coarser growths with flowers the size of marbles; the scent was delicious—far nicer than that of the acacia which mimosa otherwise resembles.

The farmsteads here are composed mostly of wire and galvanized sheets just as they are in South Africa. I noticed that there were thousands of trees which had been cut off about two feet from the ground—I must enquire about these. I did not see any decent saddle-horses, all that I saw were either light or heavy draught-horses still with their winter coats on. The roads were remarkably good for a considerable distance from Adelaide, but apparently after about thirty miles out of the city they get worse and worse; however, the ones on which we travelled were better than those we experienced in South Africa.

On Monday a few of us went out to the Holdens for tea and

afterwards we took the girls to the theatre. Mrs. Holden was quite a nice person, I would imagine her to be very ambitious but not vulgarly so. The house was very nice, fine lofty rooms furnished for the most part in a dignified style but spoilt, I considered, by some of the ornamental chairs in the drawing-room; one of the bedrooms had some of the most handsome furniture that I have ever seen, it was made in grey satinwood. We had asparagus sandwiches of a kind that I have never tasted before; also at dinner we had some remarkably fine raisins, grapes and oranges, all of which are grown in large quantities around Adelaide.

It was a treat to ride in a Rolls again, but I was not struck with the design of the body, it was a six-light staggered saloon and the windscreen pillar badly obstructed the view. The local trains are uncomfortable, dirty and slow. In the town the traffic is controlled very well and there are a lot of police on motorcycles.

The stevedores have been working better here than at Fremantle, their cargo was certainly easier to handle but the first load was only twenty-five minutes coming ashore.

MELBOURNE

August 31st

Arrived at Port Melbourne at about seven o'clock and after about an hour we caught the train into the city which took about seven minutes. The first thing that struck me was the likeness of Melbourne to the pictures that I have seen of American cities, only Melbourne is much smaller. Perhaps next comes the traffic, it is fast and dense but controlled very well.

Right-angled crossings are very frequent, and cars wishing to turn to the right have to turn into the crossroads and slightly towards their intended street so that when the traffic is released they are the first away—I believe that in London cars go into the centre to wait. The pedestrians are also controlled, they have to recognize the left-hand rule, there are white lines on the pavements and the pedestrians must only cross the road at right-angles and not diagonally. Safety zones are provided for the tramcar passengers, some trams work on a cable but those working in the opposite direction are electrical. I was very impressed by the traffic control and it works splendidly.

The buildings vary in size and style, some fine ones are built in solid stone, others are of brick and plaster in a severe style with straight lines and plenty of windows. Some of the finest buildings are Craig's

Store, the Post Office and the Mutual and National Bank.

I am now beginning to realise the full labour difficulties in this country; there was trouble here one night as a gang of stevedores wanted full pay although they had only worked 2½ hours and had been stopped by rain—if they were not paid the full nights pay the work would be declared black and the next night's gang of stevedores would not work; this would mean the ship spending another twenty-four hours in port and all duty has to be paid. A crisis must shortly be reached in Queensland, it is the worst state. Today I hear that even the Labour premier has refused to be dictated to by the unions, this may be the start of some great upheaval which may ultimately lead to some good. Can such a situation be handled in such a calm manner as it was in England during the General Strike of 1926? I doubt it, but it will be interesting to watch developments. In the meantime would it be advisable to sell my Queensland Stocks?

The stuff served up at the music-halls is very poor, the audience seem to like something with a little more vulgarity and do not seem to be as appreciative as the African audiences were of a good show. The Australian is very Americanised and seems to have a lot more tolerance of the Americans than of the English, he does not regard the Englishman as a man from home as the South Africans do.

My impression of Australia so far is that she has a wonderful future with abundant resources of food and minerals and possesses practically everything to make her self-supporting: but she will never prosper continuously until she has some honest men to govern her.

The ship is getting empty now, there are twenty-five to thirty of us left and I shall not be sorry when the rest of them have gone. I may be foolish and unsociable but I cannot make myself like many of the people on board; not many of the men have anything about them, and the girls of today have gone down very much in my estimation. They have practically no modesty and plenty of cheek, and have no use for manners either amongst themselves or towards others; neither men or girls have much conversation—it would do many of them good to have a bit of work to do. I often think of the remarks of the ship's purser about the first-class passengers of today, "Money seems all that matters to them." Now I like it myself and would hate to be short of it but I would like to see it regarded as not the only thing worthwhile; it would do many young people good to have to work for their bread and butter and not just for pin-money.

Bird's eye view of Bourke Street, Melbourne.

MELBOURNE TO SYDNEY

S.S. *Nestor*
Melbourne Harbour.
2nd September, 1927

Dear /

We are now very near the end of our outward journey, and arrived here in Melbourne on Wednesday and expect to leave tomorrow for Sydney. I hope we arrive at Sydney on Tuesday morning, although we are due on Monday night, as I would like to observe Sydney Harbour from the sea. We left Adelaide at dawn so did not see much of it. The countryside around Adelaide is beautiful, rather like England except that all the trees were gums and mimosa, the latter is simply wonderful—it is one of the trees I have always wanted to see and shall never forget. We did not see any big farms and those that we did see consisted mostly of corrugated iron, but the cattle and sheep on them were very fine.

Adelaide is a very nice quiet respectable place, and I should prefer to live there to any place that I have seen since leaving home. The ship is very quiet and dull now but we only have a few days of it. I shall be quite glad to leave the ship at Sydney as I am really tired of the sea at present.

Since being here we have been over the Pelaco factory, it is said to be the most up-to-date factory of its kind, and I can well believe it—it was a real eye-opener. They employ nearly 1,000 people and I never saw a better dressed or happier crowd in a factory, they might have been working for themselves by their looks; of course, all the work is quite clean, and when earning £5 per week and over they can afford to dress well. The working hours are from 8.00 a.m. to 5.00 p.m. with breaks for lunch and tea. There is a canteen, with ballroom equipped with piano, for all who care to use it; the food is simple but very good, sandwiches, bread and butter, jam, cakes and fruit. I do not know what the charge is but I know I enjoyed my lunch there as much as any meal I have had for weeks.

Every single operation that can possibly be done by machine is done, in fact there is hardly any handwork done except for cutting and pressing. One example of time-saving by machinery is the machine that puts the buttonholes in the collars, this it does at the rate of 185 dozen per day as against 45 dozen per day in an Irish factory, and each machine is only attended by one girl. The whole factory consumes about 120,000 yards of shirting a week, and there is quite a lot of ground on which they hope to extend the factory in the near future. If we had not been here Vernie and I would probably never have heard of the proposed extensions. The Polaco factory make up a considerable quantity of Luvisca and they say it wears very well but they do not use any other art silks.

We had half an hour with Mr. R., who seemed quite pleased to see us and offered to do anything he could for us. He rather shocked us by showing us some towels made in this country, and selling for less than they would in England. He then proceeded to give us half an hour's lecture on Empire Trade and about a grant for one million pounds given by the British Government to Australia to promote her goods, and yet at the same time Australia is placing enormous tariffs on imported goods from home, whether it is economically possible to produce them in this country or not. He is very disturbed about the matter and has just written home about it as no one here will listen to an importer; today, however, I was very pleased to see a film advertising Morris cars.

Films advertising cars seem to be very popular out here. I was rather staggered to read that of Australian exports, £47 million goes to Great Britain and only £7 million worth of goods goes to America and yet there are far more American cars out here. I should think that 80% are American and only 10% are British. From what I have heard, the Australians much prefer the Americans, in fact, when the American navy came over here they had a more expensive welcome than the Duke and Duchess of York did.

There is another strike starting in Queensland, but it will not seriously affect us unless it lasts for a long time. If it does last it will mean throwing 19,000 men out of work of which only 10,000 will be required in the future. The labour situation in this country has its humorous side. Imagine in England the engine-driver, fireman and guard getting out at the station to play cards with the station-master! This sort of thing has happened several times in Queensland. There is going to be serious trouble soon up there as the labour situation worsens.

I like Melbourne immensely, there is more going on than in Adelaide. I believe that the suburbs are very nice to live in, the town covers a tremendous area and is twenty-four miles across if you include the suburbs; all Australian towns are like that, they are either tiny with nothing to them, or else they are huge.

Some of the buildings are very fine, especially those built recently. The city is laid out in square blocks but it does not shout the fact at you like Jo'burg does. There is one disadvantage of this planning however—the prevailing winds are north and south, the south wind comes over the ocean and up the centre of the town, and the north wind comes from over the desert, picks up sand and deposits it in the centre of Melbourne.

There are, I believe, huge deposits of brown coal in Queensland; at one place there is said to be a seam which is three hundred feet thick and the whole area covers 250 square miles—enough coal to supply Great Britain for 1,000 years. The quantities of fish around the coast are huge, there are 250 varieties of edible ones and yet fish is actually shipped from Liverpool and sold in Sydney at less than English price, cod is also imported here from Africa. There is a certain hardwood that is imported here; it is obtainable from Tasmania but thanks to high wages out here this kind of wood is brought from Norway.

The general opinion of people that know a little—but not much—is that Australia is a wonderful country with great natural resources and that the only handicap is the Australians: I do not agree with this view and would not express an opinion one way or another about the people. In spite of what I have heard I have come out here prepared to like the people and to try and understand their views—there is no doubt that a lot of the English views must seem foolish to foreigners and colonials.

I have not finalized my plans yet as it all depends on what business arrangements have been made for us at Sydney. I am quite ready to get busy and see and learn something after so long on the water. I do not know if I mentioned it before, but the wool-growers are kicking up a fuss against a proposed government suggestion for making art silk from spruce pulp: they say it will threaten wool-growing, which is the backbone of Australia.

I am longing to get the post again. I have had two letters which were postmarked 13th July, but I am quite ready to receive some more news, the newspapers out here are not very thrilling, and there is practically no news at all from England.

Yours John

SYDNEY

September 6th
Truly the most wonderfully situated harbour imaginable; Sydney

Harbour—or "our 'arbour" as the Sydneyites call it—has surpassed my optimistic most expectations. It must be just about the best situation in the world for a harbour. In its time it must have been very beautiful; today, in spite of being densely covered in many parts with houses, it is still very pretty.

The bridge, when it is finished, is to span the harbour at its busiest and narrowest part; it will be a quarter of a mile long and one hundred feet wide, and it is to carry four lines of trams. If it is ever completed it will be a wonderful bridge—at present it does not look as though the span can possibly be thrown across such a gap. Many people think that the money spent on the bridge will be wasted and that the ferries are adequate to deal with the traffic. They say that the money could have been better spent on irrigation; and when you think that as many as ten million sheep have been lost in times of drought, it makes you wonder whether the seven million pounds that the bridge is going to cost to build would not have been better spent in this manner.

From first impressions Sydney is a city with far more life about it than either Melbourne or Adelaide. The shops, banks and public buildings are just as fine, but as the streets are narrow one does not get quite the same impression of the architecture without looking rather closely. The thing that surprises me is—where does the money come from to build all these modern shops? Stores and shops which are really very modern, and which any provincial town in England would be proud of, are pulled down and even more up-to-date ones erected, some of which are being built seven stories high.

7th September

Today we went to the wool auction, the auction room is like all other auction rooms at the wool sales, but here the wool has been previously examined by the buyers. The auctioneers were remarkably efficient, whilst we were there 180 lots were sold in half an hour. The crop this year is thirty to forty pounds lighter per bale than last year and prices are correspondingly higher. There was some comment about the Russians; it is the first time they have been buyers at the wool sales and a Russian bought £15,000 worth of wool before the sale. The Japanese are not buying heavily this year owing to the uncertain state of finances in Japan. There is little demand for the lower grades but fine grades are fetching 27d per pound.

I have picked up quite a lot of useful information from Mr. Gray, the representative of Steiners, and from Broadmeadow who is Howarth's man, and also from the people I met in their company in the hotels, clubs, etc. Mr. Steiner is an Englishman who has been in this country for about six years. It seems to be a general grouse that the English manufacturers on the whole do not cater properly for the Australian market. Their chief mistake is not keeping in touch with their representing agents by themselves making periodic visits from England and for example the voiles they send out are very beautiful but they are printed in a large floral design when the present demand out here is for a simple geometric design; the same remarks apply to the art silk cloths. Another problem for anyone importing art silk from England is that they are competing against real silk from France and Japan at the lower end of the trade. There are a lot of cheap silk shirts from Japan: I even saw a shirt made of cotton which had been grown in Australia, it was quite reasonable in price and the quality was not bad.

Regarding the pattern of shirting, there seems to be no definite trend, all over effect, stripes and self colours are worn; the Australian does seem to buy more shirts than are bought at home—perhaps this is because of his habit of going without a coat.

The agents out here are very fed up with Sir Amos Nelson, for causing, or helping to cause a tariff wall to be erected around khaki drills, etc., cloth which weighs over six ounces per square yard will have to pay a duty of 1/- per yard and more. There are also conflicting rumours that Nelson is going to start manufacturing out here; one is that they are starting to build a factory in October, others say that he is not going to manufacture out here at all*.

7th September

We called to see Mr. Hymer, the manager of the Australian branch of B. & D., he had very little time for us and soon turned us over to Cook the head of the shirting department; I got the impression that Mr. Hymer did not want to talk, or more likely he did not want us to see too much and for us to go back and talk. What struck me as queer though I did not remark on it, was that B. & D. are buying our check

---

* The firm of James Nelson were cotton manufacturers and also working with art silk. They built a factory in Tasmania in 1945 which is still operating.

shirting 1699 from Tingeys and selling it under the name of Tussora. Tingeys, by the way, have a very good name out here as stockists and are considered to be up-to-date people.

I had an interview with Mr. Kershaw, the B.D.A.* representative, and he offered me his services in any way necessary, but he told me that I would learn far more about the trade in Australia by being with Vernie when he was travelling as Vernie was actually showing goods for sale. We had a long talk and he told me how he found people to deal with in business, and he also gave me some introductions. It seems that B.D.A. had written from England to him of our intended visit, which was decent of them.

I later visited various business men with Mr. Kershaw and have made notes of our calls, we were very courteously received by all of them, especially considering that they were all heads of departments and that we were neither selling cloth or showing samples.

There are a very fine lot of straight people here in the textile trade and most of them are honest. They will always see you if they are not too busy and will comment on your samples, they are however very slack about keeping appointments; they are slow buyers, it is impossible to rush them and they will not buy if they are not in a buying mood.

The wholesaler is rapidly becoming a back number except for the specialist wholesalers. The retail shops buy collectively for their departments—and judging by the size and prosperity of the shops, their system is right.

The people as a whole spend freely, too freely; a working man thinks nothing of spending 30/- on a silk shirt, wages are high, and a youth of twenty-one gets £4 12s 6d automatically; but as the cost of living is high the working man is neither worse or better off than in England. In spite of the extravagance of the people, the savings in the banks are very high per head of the population.

The workmen here are good, provided they are not agitated by the unions. The union agitators here are usually English, very few are Australian-born.

The retail shops are wonderful, especially the large stores. The men's outfitters continue to surprise me, they cater exclusively for men from head to foot. Everything is displayed in the window and the standard of window-dressing leaves the British shops cold, ties, socks, and even braces are in the window together with boots, shoes, shirts and suits. Three of the largest stores Farmers, Lous and Murdochs are all situated

*Bradford Dyers Association.

close together which is rather remarkable. The founder of one firm started up by cleaning old suits—last year their turnover was £600,000.

The men's outfitters are certainly the largest I have ever seen, and the ladies' shops are just as good. In the large stores furniture, wirelesses, photography and books are all laid out to attract and not to frighten the intending purchaser.

12th September

One day last week we visited Grace Brothers, where it is possible to buy textiles, clothing, all kinds of furnishing goods both antique and modern, engineer's tools and all sports requisites, including boats.

Grace Brothers also have a grocery store where you take your own basket and walk round collecting what you want, and the assistants check off as you go out; by this method it is possible to buy at 30% below what you would pay at an ordinary store. There is also a tea-room with cafeteria, here you collect your things at the counter and take them to your table, thus doing without waitress service and saving about 50%.

15th September

We have made quite a few more business calls about which I have made some notes to send off home. When contemplating trade out here as far as textiles go I have been thinking about Australia's position in the world; she is very much in need of population, which needs to be of the right sort; if Australia is to be kept white she must be developed now. The Japanese talk about expansion and although Manchuria would be more convenient for Japan it would be awful if she got hold of a large slice of Australia; China has a tremendous population; Italy refers to Australia as "their happy hunting ground"; and last but by no means least, America could find a very good use for Australia—already American cars are being manufactured here in large quantities, and a lot of American goods are coming in despite the tariffs; Germany is dumping goods here; and Japan is somehow sending her goods here below cost price.

The opinion of a couple of large wholesalers is that we have not much to fear from the Americans in the better cotton and silk cloths, but that the Americans are more careful about exporting prints which are suitable for that particular country. I tried to impress on the buyer at

David Jones, Sydney's largest retail store, the importance of making the public realize that most good art silks can now be washed successfully. One wholesaler, however, was of the opinion that we would lose half our dress-goods trade to the Americans unless a drastic change of manufacturing methods takes place, and I quote him as saying, "It is not that the British manufacturer, cannot, but that he will not, produce the right stuff. American designs are more up-to-date."

SYDNEY AND THE SUBURBS

20th September

The more one sees of the capital the more one marvels at the good fortune of the inhabitants. Sydney must be one of the most favoured cities for pleasure and sport in the world. Within a few minutes, and for little cost, one can get into the country or to the beaches; at the beaches there is such wonderful bathing to indulge in. Many people leave work on Saturday, go to Manly, or Bondi or one of the lesser beaches and spend the whole week-end in their bathing costumes; many take a tent and sleep out.

The great beauty of the bathing, apart from the Pacific rollers, is that you can play in and out of the water without getting cold, in fact there is a very grave danger of sunburn if due precautions are not taken.

There are look-out stations or posts on all the principal beaches, and also a life-saving club: the club is manned voluntarily by a crowd of wonderful swimmers who are always ready to risk anything to rescue a swimmer in difficulties—the number of lives which they save in a year amounts to thousands. There are also several fine swimming-baths within the harbour, they have all got shark-proof netting, and it is possible to indulge in mixed bathing all the year round.

Other attractions of Sydney are a flying ground, dirt-track and dog-racing track, there are also illuminated tennis courts.

The harbour itself contains most wonderful inlets and creeks which would take years to explore fully. Many people spend the whole week-end in their yachts or boats.

The yacht races are very popular, the eighteen-footer class probably providing the best sport: these boats have no centre-board and are very shallow, they carry a very large crew whose duty it is to keep the boat the right way up by sitting themselves on the side. There is a great deal of skill required to manage a shallow boat with a human ballast, needless to say in a strong wind all the crew are drenched with spray, they also have to be good swimmers in order to right the boat should it capsize.

A lot of people who spend the week-end in the open do so very cheaply, they do practically no cooking and live almost entirely on fresh fruit. I went on nearly all the ferries in the harbour in order to see as much as possible of the area—it was wonderful: there are many beautiful houses built on the hillside, and many have gardens reaching down to the water's edge and have their own boat-houses and bathing-pools.

There is a naval shipyard called Cockatoo Island where they are building an aircraft-carrier. The section of harbour where the Paramatta River flows into the main water is very busy, at this part there are shipyards, cooling stations and oil dumps; but apart from these the place is very beautiful. One of the advantages that this harbour has over many land-locked harbours is that all the main bays have a river emptying into them which helps to remove the refuse.

We had a beautiful run out one day as far as the Bull Look-out, this is a layer of rock far above the plain, and is about three miles from the coast. From the summit it is possible to see for twenty to thirty miles either way and the view was wonderful. Marten drove the Kings and I out, and during the day we had a very interesting discussion, it was about the possibility of the capital of the British Empire eventually being moved to Australia, and if so whether or not this capital should be situated inland. It was certainly a thought-provoking subject, and some of the following points were made: If the capital were positioned for purely defensive reasons, it should be built 1,000 miles from the sea. This would mean the opening up of new country which would be both costly and difficult in a country where there are no roads or railways. Necessary material such as coal and iron would be available, but at what cost to mine; also, labour would be difficult to obtain and even more difficult to handle once transported to the site. The advantage of being so far inland would be that it would be much simpler to defend the capital as enemy aircraft would have to travel tremendous distances over both land and sea; if the enemy used aircraft-carriers for the sea voyage these ships would be very vulnerable. The great distance from the sea would cause heavy freight and handling charges; but the modern developments in wireless would mean that there were no communication problems. Finally, although those on the dole could be used to build this experimental town, wages would have to be modified and this would cause havoc with the unions.

On another day when Marten took the Kings, Vernie and I went for a run, we made our lunch on the roadside in an orange grove; the smell was perfect. The main thing that I shall always remember about the picnic is the difficulty we had in getting enough water, which incidentally we had to buy, in order to make a can of tea. On our way back we passed through the National Park which is a game reserve, but to which the public have access under certain conditions.

We are going to go to Melbourne for a few days and have planned to go by road; it will be a very long journey. I expect we will return to Sydney by sea. Whilst I am in Melbourne I hope to visit a sheep station in the outback.

22nd September

I have just spent a very interesting dinner hour with the works manager and the sales manager of The Farmers' Implement Co., the former, a Mr. Gill, has been here for seventeen years, and could not say enough good about the country. The people of Australia he regards as straightforward, they give and take fairly, and he said that anyone can get on by working hard and dealing straight; "giving value and service" was how he put it.

Mr. Gill painted a very glowing picture of his life in this country as he travelled the backwoods; of the breakdowns and emergency repairs, of the people whom he had picked up on the road, and of the houses in which he had stayed. The life-style of the squatter or retired miner made it look as though he was worth nothing, but he probably had about £50,000 put away; as he had done without in his early life he preferred to live quietly in retirement, rather than in the city.

Of the conservatism of the British manufacturers Mr. Gill had some very hard things to say, and that they were not prepared to cater for a particular market. He did admit, however, that they were at last beginning to stir themselves by sending out representatives to this country. One interesting point he mentioned was that the most prosperous years for Australia have been under a Labour government.

I was advised not to miss the Sydney Show. I was also invited to inspect the Farmers' Implement Works, which I did a few days later.

Sydney Show was a very interesting affair, it was like any other big agricultural show but with a few extras that we do not see at home, such as wood-chopping competitions, etc. The jumping was excellent, it started with the fence at six foot, and, going up at six inches at a time, one horse cleared seven feet; this was very good indeed, considering that it was out in the open and after a shower of rain.

We spent a very pleasant evening with Arthur Roper at his home which is about ten miles from Sydney, it was lovely to see an open fire again after weeks of ships and hotels without them. Arthur Roper has a drapery store in a rapidly growing suburb of Sydney, he has also bought quite a lot of land in the main street: he should do quite well out of it.

Before leaving Sydney for Melbourne I would like to record a few completely unconnected notes which I have jotted down: Mechanical hares for greyhound-racing were first used here; Sydney is the fifth largest port of the Empire, in 1903 there were 6,000 vessels, in 1914 10,000 vessels; the Queensland strike has just ended in a victory for the premier; New Zealand £25 Perpetual Shares have become worth £500 in 20 years—swift what!

The more I see of the harbour the more I wonder at the magnificence of it, for about ten miles this side of the circular quay it seems to be deep all the way across as I have seen quite large ships go up; another advantage is that the current is practically negligible, and there is no danger of the smaller craft being washed against each other.

SYDNEY TO MELBOURNE

This was a most interesting journey by road, the only improvements could have been more room in the car, less speed, and a better driver. Looking back at it now that the journey is over I feel that on the whole I enjoyed it, and it certainly gave me an insight into driving conditions in this country. I can now understand why cars of the 12-horse class are not popular, as the roads have so many pot-holes it is necessary to crawl at a walking pace in order to save the springs—the Australian driver is lazy, he dislikes using his gear-lever and expects to be able to do this in top gear; clearance of the car must be good.

We left Sydney at about noon on Saturday, and before stopping for the night we had covered about 250 miles. The first 100 miles of the journey was over good roads which then deteriorated from bad to worse by the hour. We passed through some wonderful afforested country and enjoyed it immensely until it grew dark and we became tired. At night we stayed at a place called Eden, and slept, or tried to sleep, to the accompaniment of croaking bull-frogs, I did not realize that they could really croak like that—it was most wierd.

We left at about seven o'clock the following morning, it showed promise of being a beautiful day, after photographing a tame parrot and filling up with petrol we set off. After about two hour's motoring the petrol-tank ran dry, all the petrol had flowed back into the pump instead of the tank. Vernie and I set off to walk on ahead as we had not previously seen a petrol station for miles back. Fortunately we got some juice from a passing car which was enough to get us as far as Sans Soucci where we had breakfast. Vernie and I had thoroughly enjoyed our walk, everything had been so peaceful and still, and we would have preferred to walk some more rather than go in the car, the others, however, had come across similar experiences before, in fact, one of them used to make the journey in a coach-and-four and remembered that they used to average only four miles a day for a week.

We travelled through more or less wooded country until about 3.00 p.m. when we were held up by a bridge having been washed away, there had been a tremendous rainstorm and a lot of the countryside was under water. We saw hundreds of dead sheep that had just been newly shorn, I also saw a huge flock of cockatoo—which pleased me.

Having left the road where the bridge had been washed away, we travelled for many miles on what are known as stock routes or three-chain roads. They are not roads at all, but strips of ground which are three chains wide, and along which sheep and cattle are overlanded. There is a wire fence on either side, and the drover is bound by law to traverse four or five miles each day with his herd so that the animals do not eat the land bare for when the next drove comes along. Some of these stock routes have cart ruts running along them, but most have no track at all.

The great advantage of these routes to a driver such as ours was that he could drive without there being anything to hit. He was too clever to put chains on the wheels, or to keep going steadily in low gear. The car was a 35-horsepower Chandeler, it had a wonderful performance in top gear, but what we gained in speed we lost in the time it took getting out of the car and pushing the car round to face Melbourne instead of Sydney; after doing this for the fifth time we were a bit fed up. Finally, a farmer who had stopped to help turn the car round directed us on to another route.

We slithered and jolted about on this route until about 6.30 p.m. when we got to a village and were fortunate to obtain a meal. I think all the passengers would have liked to have stayed the night but the driver wanted to get along. We eventually got back on to a third-rate road but about an hour later came across a river running over this road. As there were no hedges to steer by I got out and waded in to see if I could find the way, I was soon in it up to my knees so we turned back. Later we learned that at this place the flood had been half a mile wide and over five feet deep. We tried yet another road and after fixing the chains on and traversing through water which was several feet deep for about 600 yards, we reached a bridge over which the water was only just starting to rise and managed to get across and soon found a house in which to stay the night. We had been motoring from 7.00 a.m. to 11.30 p.m.

At noon the following day we arrived in Melbourne having covered 760 miles since Saturday noon. I have never been more thankful to finish a motor journey, we had all had enough, but it had been a wonderful experience and I should not have liked to have missed it.

BURRAMBUT SHEEP STATION

I spent a marvellous week-end at Burrambut, Mr. A. Currie's station, the place is about 100 miles from Melbourne and is ten miles from the nearest station. The house is a copy of an old Scottish mansion and is beautifully situated in a real English garden with English trees and plants: there were huge wide lawns, fish-ponds, and a fish hatchery. The fish-ponds were also inhabited by thousands of bullfrogs which made the night hideous with their croakings, however, one soon gets used to it. The interior of the house is beautifully furnished and must have cost a small fortune in antiques, especially the collection of swords and pistols. In the garden is an old wellhead which has at one time been brought from Egypt or Palestine, at the time the disputed ownership of it nearly led to serious trouble between the governments.

At home, I have always looked down on sheep, out here I cannot help but admire these fine animals which incidentally keep themselves very clean.

At one time the estate extended across all the four hills, and covered 1,800 square miles. In those days it was marked out in the good old method of ploughing up a double furrow of earth and claiming the land inside. Today only about 9,000 acres is owned by the Curries but it is probably one of the most valuable stations of the Australian continent. It raises about 12,000 sheep and 250 head of cattle, also fifty to sixty horses of all sorts; from race-horses to cart-horses, polo ponies and quiet hacks. The sheep here are ones that are mainly used for experimental breeding, the bulk of the flock is kept at the Currie's other station in South Australia which extends to 2,000 square miles.

I was not there in time for shearing, but did get a certain amount of riding across the estate watching the men at work sorting the sheep and lambs, etc. One afternoon I spent with the foreman boundary riding; this is the inspection of the station for injured sheep, gaps in the fences, and keeping an eye open for snakes. The only snakes we saw were dead ones, but because of them a boundary rider always carries a rifle on his rounds. The foreman had an interesting tale to tell. His father had been overlanding cattle in Queensland at the time of the gold-rush, he set off to make his way here and the journey had taken him eighteen months, by the time he got to the camp here the rush was over and the camp was deserted, so they then started up this sheep station on this same spot. Overlanding cattle is a most wonderful way of seeing the country; if I could write of what I saw I would certainly try doing a trip with a herd—but it takes many months.

I spent one afternoon walking with a couple of dogs and a stout ash-stick, I turned over many stones looking for snakes and I would have got a shock if I had seen one,—I did, however, find a couple of guana lizards which were ten to twelve feet long, they make a very hideous spectacle with a vivid red head only slightly less in size than their green body. Another interesting sight was a colony of bull ants, they were similar to our own brown ants, but much larger. I saw for the first time in my life jack hares boxing, I have often read of them doing it, especially in March, but never had the good fortune to see them.

I do not think I have ever enjoyed riding more than I have done here, where the wild life is so completely different to what we see at home: we certainly do not see laughing jackasses, red and green parrots, white cockatoos, and large eagles, when we ride in the country. The view from the hill at the back of the house was magnificent, to me the hill appeared to overlook a stretch of country as big as Yorkshire.

MELBOURNE

Soon after getting back to Melbourne we went to Myers Department Store, it is the biggest department store south of the line. There is a very large department selling piece goods, and it employs 400 hands,

Flinders Street Railway Station, Melbourne.

only thirty of them are selling cotton dress goods, the rest are selling silk and silk dress materials, also shirting and casements.

One day we visited a weaving shed a few miles from Melbourne: it was a treat to hear a loom again; if I had to live in Australia I should certainly consider having a loom put in the garden so that I could hear the clatter occasionally. This mill was run on very crude lines, but in spite of the fact that there were only forty looms it should be a little gold-mine, considering all the protection the textile industry gets in this country. I was interested to see the goods being handled by lifting-trucks. Most of the power for the looms is supplied by the local corporation. This juice is cheaper than the Queensland brown coal which is used for heating.

Back in Melbourne I met Fink, an old schoolfriend of mine, he is employed as an advertising artist and seems pretty satisfied with life. We were talking about the relative price of things out here: fruit is very cheap and seems to be sold in large quantities, so is honey which is advertised a great deal, but everything that is imported is very expensive. It is impossible to judge the quality of the Japanese Fugi silks from outside the shop windows but they seem to be very cheap, as are leather goods. Certain cotton and silk goods seem to be reasonably priced.

I thought things more expensive than in Sydney where I had bought half a dozen neckties, they were only about 4/6d and were quite good ones, in fact it had been impossible to pay more. Whilst I was at it I also bought a number of presents, mostly for the family, and they included two ornamental boomerangs, two proper boomerangs, and a stock-whip for Reg.

During the return trip to Sydney from Melbourne by sea, I was fortunate enough to drop across a cousin of Ronald Angus, it was a rather remarkable coincidence that she should be at our table in the dining-room and was one of only half a dozen people that I spoke to on the trip. She promised to let Angus know that I would soon be in Sydney, and to see that I met him.

I have decided to go to New Zealand, and shall go as soon as I can get a sailing from Sydney and should be back sometime in early November.

WELLINGTON, NEW ZEALAND

The Grand Hotel, Wellington.

If this crossing was a fair sample of New Zealand crossing, I can quite understand why so few Australians visit this country and *vice versa*. For a whole four days it was bitterly cold, and the sea was so rough that at times it was impossible to stand up. I only ever saw about seventy passengers, but discovered when looking at the list at Wellington, that there were 140 on board. The first glimpse we had of the South Island was at about 7.00 a.m., the coastline looked beautiful in the morning light, the distant hills were shrouded in a purple haze and many of them were capped in snow.

I was not impressed with Wellington Harbour as we entered it, within two hours of having seen beautiful scenery we ran into a heavy rainstorm which continued until we landed. As it had been with our arrivals at Adelaide, Melbourne and Sydney, so it cleared as soon as we stepped ashore. Looking through the mist and drizzle towards the

General View, Wellington, New Zealand.

harbour, I thought of a Scottish lake on a dull day. Within a couple of hours I had discovered that the harbour is very beautiful with the background of distant mountains.

Wellington is not a very impressive city, but the more one looks the more one finds in the way of good buildings. The city is only eighty years old and is built at the bottom of a cliff, most of the land on which it has been built is land reclaimed from the harbour, a process which is still going on steadily. The houses are mostly of wood on account of the shortage of good building stone, and also, to some extent, on account of the danger of earthquakes. The shops are not to be compared to the Australian ones, I like this feature of the town it makes it seem less American.

I visited the New Zealand Preference Exhibition and was pleased to note the variety of products on display that were made in New Zealand; iron and steel goods made from iron mined in this country; brass, tin ware and light castings; several forms of simple light-weight machinery; soaps, pastes, polishes, matches and clothing. The most interesting stands were those of the woollen mills where the garment is made from the raw wool; it is scoured, dyed, and woven on the spot; some of the suiting being made were very nice, the rugs were of excellent quality and have a world-wide name.

I had a few meals at the same table as the manager of one of the woollen mills, I was sorry I could not get to know him a little better, but as I only saw him for a few hours I could hardly ask him point blank for an invitation to inspect his mill.

Whilst at Wellington I visited a little village called Hutt, it reminded me of Church Stretton except that it had quite a large stream flowing through it. The scenery was very English, the dusty roads and dense hedgerows, and birds which resembled the thrush and the blackbird in their call. On the way back I went by the harbour road. It is a very fine motor road which runs round Wellington Harbour, which is enclosed on three sides and the road seems to run very close to the edge of the water, it is about eighteen miles long.

The following day I went to Napier by train. I thoroughly enjoyed the journey along rivers, past mountains and through pasture-lands where the cattle and sheep grazed contentedly in luxurious green grass; in the background were farmsteads, often crude but very picturesque, many with weeping willows round them—such a change from the stark gum trees of Australia.

I had left Wellington hurriedly for Napier, and in my haste left one of my cases in the taxi. I had to stay another day in Napier to wait for my bag, but the stay was well worthwhile. I visited Havelock and Hastings, walking through some real country lanes which might have been ten miles from home, I took some photos and bought others when I got back to Napier. It is quite a flourishing port, and it is the centre of prosperous farming country.

WAIRAKEI

The following day I left Napier by motor for Wairakei, the country soon changed from pastoral land to wild, wooded hills; it was necessary to climb these quite slowly and steadily, but we made up for lost time going down the slope.

On examining the visitors' book at the Wairakei Hotel I saw that three Englishmen had been staying there but it did not occur to me to ask whether or not they had left; their names were Langlen, Lonsdale and Smith. I went into the smoke-room and one of them was talking in quite a refined way, he could not always keep clear of his Lancashire accent so I asked him where he came from, and found that he knew Harold quite well. If I had stayed at Taupo the night, as I had been tempted to, I should have missed them, and what turned out to be one of the most enjoyable periods of my life.

From Wairakei I visited the Huka Falls and also the Aratitia Rapids, neither are very big, but although the depth of fall is not great there is a tremendous amount of water flowing over them. At night we went to the Blow-hole, it is a hole of only about six inches in diameter through which steam blows at a pressure of 180lb., and has done for the last two centuries; a very wierd effect can be obtained by placing a smouldering rag in the steam-jet, sparks are sent up to a tremendous height and the steam-jet looks like an enormous firework. If the steam could be harnessed it would yield a tremendous amount of power, the land around the hole is not strong enough to support machinery.

The following morning we went to the Geyser Valley, it was most interesting but I have no desire to go there again: it is most unsafe to walk anywhere except on the path, and even then it is hardly safe without a guide. There were many active geysers to see, some of them are continuously active, others at regular periods.

There is the Champagne Pool so called because the cascade of water sparkles like champagne; others have names such as the Helium Pool, the Paddle-wheel Pool, Dancing Rock, Dragon's Mouth and the Crow's-nest Geyser; there is also a waterfall called the Golden Waterfall which runs over golden-coloured rocks so formed by the deposits left by the water, and another smaller one named the Pink Terrace.

After a bathe in the hot swimming-pool followed by a cold plunge I felt very refreshed, and in the afternoon some of us visited the Waiora Valley where we saw the mudpools, some were comparatively cold, others boiling; most of them were white or grey; but some were red, blue and green. A thing that struck me as remarkable was that the trees and other shrubs that grow around these pools and geysers do not seem to be affected by the sulphur fumes. At night I phoned the Landlass party at Taupo to arrange some fishing, and after a very dull evening I went to bed early.

TAUPO

The following morning it rained hard, and I doubted whether we would be able to fish from a launch. At breakfast I found that the young man I was speaking to was a friend of Carter who was at Burton Bank with me and we had quite an interesting talk.

I got to Taupo in good time, and we started from the quay at about ten o'clock. The weather cleared slightly, and although it continued to drizzle—and did so the whole time—I would not have liked to have missed the day: apart from the fishing the view of the hills from the far side of the lake was wonderful, and on that account alone the day was worthwhile. We caught about twenty fish of an average weight of 5lb., and, although I only landed three myself, I had plenty of excitement with those I did catch—and with the big ones that escaped!

The boatman was a good type of fellow for the job, and seemed as anxious for a successful day as we were: he made us a delicious meal of trout, the best fish I have ever tasted. The wind got up after lunch so we had to fish in the bays near the lake-side, and even then we got quite a tossing. We returned to the hotel at about six o'clock for another trout meal, and then as we were very tired we went to bed very early.

The following day was bright, and before setting off for another day's fishing I wrote to Gwen Kenrick and to Billie to tell them that I was sending them some fish. Owing to the transport facilities not being all they might be, except between big towns, I thought it might be advisable to warn them that the fish would be on their way. I had counted my chickens a bit too soon as we only caught one fish all morning, it was not surprising as we could see the bottom in places as deep as twenty-five to thirty feet: this fish we ate for lunch. It was not until the sun became overcast at 2.30 p.m. that the fish started to bite, and between then and 6.00 p.m. we caught twenty-six fish of which I caught seven. Altogether it had been very cheap sport, as my expenses including the licence, launch and hotel bill, had worked out at 2/6d per lb of fish.

ROTORUA

We motored to Rotorua on Thursday and thorougly enjoyed the run. The New Zealand bush country is denser and more picturesque than the Australian bush, and parts of the undergrowth are quite impenetrable without an axe. The tree ferns are very beautiful, about a hundred varieties of them grow on the island, from dwarf ones to trees that are forty feet high or more. Of the creepers perhaps the most interesting one is the Mungo-Mungo which sticks to anything and everything: it is very springy and on that account is used by the bushmen for filling their sleeping bags. One of the smaller types of tree has leaves with a white underside and these are used by bushmen to indicate the way that they have travelled, they simply turn over a leaf and point it in the right direction.

We arrived at about 3.00 p.m. at Rotorua, and almost as soon as I had entered the hotel the hall porter told me that he had someone staying from Nelson about six years ago! We all went round the geysers and the Maori village with Rangi, who is a most entertaining guide. In the village we saw what was probably the original centrally-heated house, a geyser had started under the house so the water and steam had been led away underneath in pipes. We saw Maoris cooking, and washing themselves and their clothes in concrete pools which were fed by natural hot springs. We saw many geysers, one of which will always start to play if a bar of soap is thrown in it, another one plays in the middle of a cold stream; here it is possible to catch a fish, and without lifting it out of the water drag it into the geyser and boil it.

We were taken to a model Maori village, built, of course, for the benefit of the visitors. Rangi was most interesting, and explained to us in detail the Maori carvings, and the origin of the figures having hands with only three fingers which occur in almost all Maori decorations.

On Friday we did the round trip which included taking a rowing boat across two lakes, one deep blue and the other deep green: one of the lakes, whilst quite cool in the centre was almost boiling at one side. We again drove through some magnificent bush country. The more I see of the New Zealand bush the more I like it, the great beauty of it is that it is free of such reptiles as snakes and the like. We passed quite close to Rainbow Mountain which is of volcanic origin, it looks almost like sandstone and is most beautifully coloured. One of the valleys along which we walked was fearfully hot, and there were hot springs and streams all along it. Perhaps most impressive of all was the crater of the greatest of all the geysers, Wumungo, which when active used to hurl mud, stones and water to a height of 1,500 feet, but which for many years has remained dormant. We also saw Tarawera the last of the volcanoes to blow up, and the one that buried the famous pink terraces.

We had a fine drive on Saturday partly along the Hongi Track, one of the legendary routes used by the last Maori chiefs when the white men tried to take the country. We saw many lakes of various colours, one of which rose and fell periodically for no apparent reason.

On Sunday the others played golf with the New Zealand lady champion, as Smith and I do not play we walked round with them. It was quite an interesting course and it was surprising how a boiling mudpool puts people off playing quite a short shot. After lunch Smith and I went to the Fairy Spring where there were more trout than I thought possible in so small a space. The spring enters Lake Rotorua via a stream, one side of this stream was alive with trout, but quite big fish of five to ten pounds were being kept to one side by a fish known as the sergeant fish, he would not allow any of the trout on to his side of the stream.

AUCKLAND

Vernie had to be getting on with his work, so we went to Auckland on Monday. As he was sailing for Sydney on the following day, and I wanted to spend a few more days in New Zealand I arranged to sail on the *Marama* to Sydney in a couple of days time. I was intending to phone Billie later in the day on Tuesday, but she came into The Star for lunch, she looked sweeter than ever and I felt quite bucked that she seemed pleased to see me; she asked me over to her home for lunch the

Queen Street, Auckland, New Zealand.

following day. At night Vernie and the other party left for Sydney, and by the time they were on board it was time for me to go to bed.

I went to the Martin's place the next day at Wiri, it is about fifteen miles from Auckland, from the appearance of it I got the impression that their farm must have fallen on hard times in recent years. We went for a nice run in the afternoon, and at night Billie, her sister, a friend and I went to the pictures. Thursday morning I had a look round Auckland, and in the afternoon went to the golf club to have tea with Billie. We had a great rush to get back to Auckland in time for dinner as we had to change first. Billie was again looking very nice in black. After dinner we went to see *The Cradle Snatchers,* not a bad show, though I thought it a bit outspoken in parts but we enjoyed it immensely. After the theatre four others joined us, and having consumed a few drinks at the hotel, we went out and had a ham and egg supper at midnight. Perhaps it was as well that there was a crowd when we said good-bye; it made it informal at any rate. Billie would not promise to see me off on the following day although I did my best to persuade her.

11th November

The ship sailed at 3.00 p.m. prompt, and consequently I did not see Billie; greatly disappointed. There were few people on board the *Marama,* and if I had not been on this ship previously I should have had a very thin time of it indeed; as it was, I was fortunate enough to be able to spend some time on the bridge with the first mate as we sailed out of Auckland Harbour.

I became quite friendly with a few members of the company who had just finished playing *The Ghost Train* in Auckland and who were travelling back to Sydney. In spite of this the trip was dull; the sea was fairly calm although many people were ill, and there was not a decent looking girl on board.

15th November

As soon as I arrived back in Sydney I booked my passages on the *Taiping* and *Hector* and the *Antenor.* I am leaving Vernie in Sydney on 18th December, and will not meet up with him until March in Ceylon. Before I leave for the East, however, I hope to spend a week in Adelaide. I shall go by train and return by sea.

20th November

Had a busy week in Sydney and made some notes for Harold, went to the races at Banwick, and this morning went surfing on Manly Beach for about an hour, then met Landlass and Co. at the club to have tea with them: at night I wrote letters.

The Commercial Travellers' Association Club

27 Martin Place,

Sydney.

20th November, 1927

Dear Harold and Gertrude,

I was very glad to get your letter last week, but was so busy that I had no time to reply to it properly.

I have definitely booked my passage to Hong Kong and Singapore, and then from Colombo home. The ship on which I shall be travelling in the Far East is the S.S. *Taiping,* she is only 4,000 tons and is owned by a Chink firm. Whilst I feel that I ought to support home industries I cannot afford to wait here another two months for a British sailing. On this ship I shall have the chance of coming into contact with a few Japanese and Chinese, and I think it advisable to do so.

We reach Hong Kong on 7th January, and I leave there on the 25th, subject to confirmation of my cable for accommodation out there. Between these two dates—if I have any luck at all I shall be able to visit Nagasaki and Yokohama, in any case I can spend some time in Shanghai, but will have little time to do much at the other ports.

It will be 31st January before I get to Singapore, and from there I shall go to India. As I do not have to be in Colombo to meet up with Vernie until the 4th March I shall have quite reasonable time to visit Rangoon, Calcutta and Madras, but Bombay is out of the question altogether. The only way I can get more time in China and Japan is to omit India from the trip, well, I think the latter more important and have booked "according-lie" (as Jimmy would say). By the way, I will look his brother up in Madras. If you think otherwise, wire me, c/o Butterfield and Lever Ltd., Hong Kong.

I shall be very busy from now until I leave Sydney. Tomorrow I go to the Blue Mountains and the Janolan Caves, the trip takes three days. On Friday I shall go to Canberra, as a white elephant it should be quite interesting. I then go on by train to Melbourne, and to Adelaide where I have an invitation to stay. I also have Hance's friend, Ronald Angus, to look up. I should be back in Melbourne by 10th December but would like to be there a couple of days before, especially if the cloth samples have arrived: I hope you have sent them off as I have had no reply.

The *Taiping* will call at about four Queensland ports, so by rushing about a bit I should see something of that part of the country, I wish, however, that we could get a couple of days in Brisbane instead of only a few hours.

Well, to get back to your letter, I see you are still increasing your range of silks. Mr. Grey, Steiner's man, was asking me if we used silk in the cloth which we supply to them, I said I had forgotten which sample number it was, but I am pretty sure he knew all about it.

Yesterday we went to the races, and although we did not win, we only lost 30/- between us so we did not feel badly done by and we had a good run for our money. The day was perfect, the sort of weather that we could probably make £700 to £800 at Gisburn Races. (I shall probably be home in time.) The concrete was uncomfortable to walk on and the seats were hot to sit on, but there was a slight breeze so it was not too bad.

I was struck by the absence of voiles being worn, as the shops have a lot in; I only saw about four altogether. Out here silk and art silk have it all their own way, I made a note of the designs and colours, they varied greatly; there were also a lot of plain colours, the wine shades being very beautiful. I now know why we did not make money with our designs out here, it was the wrong form we studied!

The enclosed cutting will interest you—if I do not forget to enclose it. You will, of course, have heard all about the new factory that British Celanese are building out here, the silk they spin is to be used in the hosiery trade. Out here silk is landed at only 5/- to 6/- : if the factory is as big as we hear that it is they will soon be producing too much. They will, of course, be protected by a tariff wall over which it will be impossible to climb.

I am very sorry to hear that Gertrude's head is still not better, I do hope the man in Harrogate can do some good, it is so disappointing going on week after week like this. Reg will be feeling very pleased with himself for winning all his cups (and saucers), you will need an extra room at Moorlands. I suppose you will all be moved in by now, well, if you are not, I hope you have done so by April as my trunk will take up a bit too much space in the cottage.

It is a pity that Mouse has turned out a bit too hot for Reg, perhaps she may not be when she is actually hunting. I am very glad to hear that you have sent Countess down to Hance, she certainly needed sharpening up before I left and I shall need her to be right for when I get back home—I shall have forgotten how to sit on a horse. I hope to get a bit of riding this coming week when I am in Adelaide, in fact, I hope to get some riding every day. I was to have had a ride when I was in Auckland, but when we caught one of the horses he was minus a shoe, "and so the poor Pommy had none".

Well, I must close now, when you get this the sleet and snow will probably be falling on you at the same speed as the sweat runs out of me as we sail up the Queensland coast.

Love from,
John.

Jenola Caves, Sydney
23rd November, 1927
Post card to—Master Reg Hindley,
Moorlands.

Dear Reg,

I am just having a couple of days at the caves, they are really wonderful. The Wallabies in the picture are a small species of kangaroo; they are really wild, but will come down to the house to feed at night.

Cheerio,
John.

Jenola Caves, Sydney
23rd November, 1927
Post card to—Mrs. H. Hindley,
Moorlands.

Dear Gertrude,

The colourings of the caves are really wonderful, pure white with bronze and mahogany. The caves were rather tiring to visit, yesterday I climbed 2000 steps.

Hope you are all well.

Love from,
John.

Canberra,
24th November, 1927
Post card to—Mrs. H. Hindley,
Moorlands.

Dear Gertrude,

So glad to hear that you have been better these past few weeks (since Oct. 17th).

I have just visited Canberra, there is absolutely *Nothing* to see.

I expect to be home by April, but may have to stay here indefinitely if the shipping trouble gets any worse.

Love to all,
John.

SYDNEY

Monday   *21st November*

Started for the Blue Mountains and Jenola Caves, the mountains were very fine but not equal to the scenery of Natal except that they possess a wonderful blue haze. I had a very good time at the caves, they were extremely fine and well worth a visit. There were a few rock wallabies which were very tame and came to feed out of the kitchen scrap-bin.

I returned from the Blue Mountains to Sydney on Wednesday, and on Friday morning I left for Canberra by road. I sat next to an English nurse and to Theodore the ex Labour premier of Queensland. He had nothing to say except to curse the weather—which needed it, the car was a big Hudson and we had covered 200 miles before six o'clock. Theodore is the man who changed the electoral map and moved men from one district to another at election time, he also kept an illegal two-up school, and is charged with fraud over some mining shares. He retired after getting his head into the noose, but before it tightened; today he is playing at Federal politics.

25th November

There was nothing much to see at Canberra except the official buildings they say it is to be a show-place (I have made a few notes in my small notebook). I left Canberra on Saturday night by train and travelled with a political cove; he was very interesting, in fact, I thoroughly enjoyed the journey. I met Palmer of *The Ghost Train* company in the refreshment room at Goulburn, at another stop,

Albury, I met Warwick and his wife; they are also travelling to Melbourne. We talked about my intention to visit India and they advised me that the only way to see India was overland by train.

The South Australian Commercial Travellers'
and
Warehousemen's Association Inc.

North Terrace,
Adelaide.
28th November, 1927

Dear Harold,

Just a line in case I have no time later this week. There is trouble at present with the waterside workers, and I may be delayed in Australia indefinitely: even if we only sail a few days late it will give me very little time in Hong Kong.

Yesterday I met a man who had toured the East for twenty years, he said that Japan was hardly worth visiting unless I had plenty of time, having only a few days to spare he advised me to stick to China.

He is the second knowledgeable person who has advised me to see India by train. I have been warned that it will be intensely hot and probably most uncomfortable, but it would be a wonderful chance of actually seeing India and not just the ports.

I have been very busy lately, I visited the Blue Mountains and the caves. I came down here by train from Canberra—about which more later—I arrived here about 10.00 a.m. after only a few hours stop in Melbourne, so I was quite ready for a hot bath when I got here.

Well, I must close now, hope you are all well.

Love to all,
John.

ADELAIDE

8th December

I have had quite an enjoyable week here having had an interesting but tiring train journey from Canberra, I only had three hours in Melbourne, there was just time for lunch at the club, and the train left again at 4.30 p.m. I have been riding, playing a little polo, visiting the art gallery, etc. I also spent four days at the cricket match. On Sunday I went out to Angaston, I was a bit disappointed that I could not stay with the Bowmans as they had a full house, however, I stayed at the

Angaston Hotel and have been out with them quite a lot, so it was quite worth going.

I leave for Melbourne at 1.30 today, there has been a delay in the sailing but I should still get a few calls made there before setting off for Sydney.

South Australian Commercial Travellers,
and Warehouseman's Association

North Terrace,
Adelaide
8th December,1927

Dear Reg,

I have just remembered that it will be your birthday soon, so had better write and wish you a very happy one before it is too late. What is it to be this year? A motor bike, a piano or a row of houses.

You are fourteen this time, aren't you? It does not seem long since I was myself; I expect you will be ready for four looms shortly and I suppose you would be wanting to weave horse-rugs or horsehair. I hear you have been doing a bit more mug hunting, cups I mean, not playing Red Indians.

I am leaving here today by train to catch my ship at Melbourne she has not left Sydney yet owing to the strike but is expected to sail in a couple of days. I sail from Melbourne to Sydney, and after I have spent a couple of days in Sydney I go off by myself. The *Taiping* goes round the north-west ports, Brisbane, Rockhampton, Townsville and Cairns; and then to Thursday Island which is a tiny dot on the north-west tip of Australia.

From there I go to Manila, Hong Kong, Shanghai and Singapore. As I shall have six weeks from leaving Singapore until I need to be back in Ceylon, I shall probably travel to India by train. How much I see of China and Japan after leaving Manila will depend entirely on whom I meet and what advice I can get from them, but I have arranged nothing definite.

I have visited some friends near Adelaide and done some riding, although I was a bit disappointed that I could not stay with them. If you had been with me I would have considered taking a few horses back, but they are rather a trouble to send as you cannot put them in an envelope very well.

The horses out here are wonderfully cheap. The Bowmans have a pony they only paid five pounds for, it is quite a good sort, and as a child's pony its manners are worth £50 alone. It was possible to pull it about any way, to sit on it and to slide off over its tail. If it was possible to pick up a load like that anyone could pay their expenses out of it.

Well, I am glad your two-year-old has turned out a success and hope you have some more wins next season. Are you going to hunt yet or leave it another year or so? If you do start I suppose going back to school will be worse than ever: I could do with a few days hunting myself at present, though not in this weather. The weather has been poor here for a couple of days, but today is as hot as Wigan.

I must close now, hoping that you are keeping quite well and having a good term. I enclose a few stamps which may be useful to exchange with a whip, or piece of elastic, or a set of chestnuts.

Cheerio,
John.

SYDNEY

17th December

The *Taiping* is due to sail tomorrow. I had a busy few days in Melbourne and saw Whelan, Myers and Ropner and did a bit of business, I also looked up Fink again and spent most of the week-end in his company.

I sailed for Sydney on Tuesday, the ship left Melbourne at 8.30 p.m. I had bought a pipe and could not get it going even after using thirty matches, I was more successful the following day and enjoyed it; I have smoked it ever since and never found that it tasted too strong except when smoked very fast.

THE QUEENSLAND COAST

I spent a very busy few hours in Sydney, saw several representatives, and also got some patterns of Jap' silks, and some silk and cotton American ones. I got no change at David Jones, but at Barkers, Syd quite opened up and showed me all round the place.

Did a few bits of shopping and left many things "undid" and calls unpaid but it could not be helped. We sailed at noon on Saturday, I wish Vernie had been coming but he could not. It was a very busy day in port as there were many ships leaving at the same time as we did.

Fifty Chinese stowaways have been found on board and the Dutch skipper has been fined £5,000; apparently they were smuggled on board at Fremantle.

I had been having rather a quiet time until I got into conversation with Captain Beale, he has been very interesting to talk to all the way up the coast, and has improved the journey immensely for me.

There is not much to be seen between Sydney and Brisbane except for a few headlands. We arrived at Brisbane on Monday at nine o'clock and left at 4.30 p.m. I looked round the town, bought some postcards, and caught the tram to One Tree Hill and walked up it. From the top I had a good view but a poor lunch, I must have lost some weight from the latter—and the walk no doubt did me some good. I also took some photos which have been quite successful.

I do not think much of Brisbane as a city but the surrounding country looks very nice, if only we had time to see some of it. I saw many very fine butterflies that were in beautiful colours, black white and fawn; also a few lizards, and many grasshoppers or crickets, they make a terrific row.

The people of Brisbane were rather hefty, especially the women, none of them seem to realize that it is hot and the men wear winter clothing.

We were at Townsville by Thursday morning and did not leave until Friday afternoon. I had a good walk round the town in the morning and did a little shopping, and went part way up the hill and took some photos. At night most of us, if not all of us, went to see the motor cycle races, there was some good riding and plenty of excitement and a few spills, there was a nasty bump at the finishing-post which affected most of the riders. A fellow called Salt Bush Bill gave a demonstration of whip-cracking—his only really good effort was flicking the ash out of his own cigarette. The goat-races were certainly funny, and really quite good sport, the races being a quarter-mile handicap.

On Friday morning I went with the doctor's boys to the baths in Townsville, I had quite a good time and got slightly singed but I do not seem to make much progress with my swimming. I had quite a number of dives from a couple of feet and eventually tried a dive of four feet, the first was not pleasant and when half way in I wished myself back on the bank, but after that I enjoyed them. We had a good look at all the other ships in the harbour before boarding the *Taiping*, and sailed after lunch.

S.S. *Taiping*
18th December, 1927

Dear Harold,

I am now travelling alone for a few months, I expect to meet Vernie in about March in Colombo. I don't mind it myself as I shall be too busy to feel lonely, but I feel rather sorry for Vernie as it is not very pleasant being alone in the evenings and at week-ends, but we cannot manage it any other way.

Thanks for the cuttings, I was a week late getting them and they were too late to be of much benefit I'm afraid, on my way back from Adelaide I only had a couple of days in Melbourne, and the same in Sydney.

I enclose two samples that I got in Sydney that I thought would interest you, the Japanese silk is very cheap; the other silk and cotton fabric was made in America, every manufacturer in England is supposed to have tried to match it in price, etc., and failed, so see what you can do. These samples of ours have taken everyone's fancy but they want to know the price at which they can buy our cloth finished in Manchester.

I have summarized most of what I have seen as regards prices, and of the reception that our samples have had. When I was talking to the shirting man at Hymens of Brisbane he surprised me with the news that Mr. Barlow of B. & J. is expected out here in July. I hope it is true as I'm sure they will benefit enormously by a visit from him, I have mentioned already how many wholesalers are going out of business, the retailers, especially of the larger stores, are buying direct: I think he ought to come out and see things for himself. *You might come with him.*

I expect I will have a lot of news in the next few months, though not much of it will be business. Tell Gertrude that I have just received her letter of 29th October and will write soon.

Today I have just sent you off a copy of the *Textile Journal* to Bankfield, it is published in this country. Tell Myers that I have received his letter of the 26th and will reply soon.

Love to all, John.

BRISBANE TO CAIRNS

S.S. *Taiping*
20th December, 1927

Dear Gertrude,

I was very glad to get your letter dated 29th October, and to know that you are keeping better. I hope that you are able to get to Arnside for half-term.

You mention in your letter the schools which you have tried. I suppose you will be sending Reg away in September '28 or January '29. I would consider September to be the better time wherever he goes, as there is always a crowd of new boys then in every school.

You ask if Reg will like Mill Hill as well as Bootham; well, for the first few weeks he may not, but I am quite sure that by the end of his first term he will. Of course, I should naturally like him to go, but I have tried to consider it from an unbiased point of view.

If he were going in for a profession or nothing at all Malborough, Wellington or Charterhouse I would consider the best, and I would give preference to Charterhouse. Failing those, I would consider Oundle was suitable for a profession or anything else. As these four are barred, then I would say Mill Hill, I have nothing against any other school but I do know Mill Hill. I would recommend him to be entered for "Burton Bank" or "Winterstoke" (the new house), but I should like to go down there and see for myself first. On no account enter him for "Ridgeway House", I do not consider it at all suitable.

The only objection that I have about Mill Hill being that it is, or rather was, it is possible to have a lazy time and do little work, but I am quite confident that this will in no way affect Reg, and that things will have tightened up considerably since Jacks has found his feet there properly.

I don't think you need to have the slightest worry about sending Reg to a big school, I am quite sure that he is just as fit if not fitter than the majority of boys that go away. What a pity he could not have spared the time from school to come out here with me, it would have done him the world of good to get all this sun.

We are having rather a dull trip at the moment, but the sea and the weather are perfect. The people on board are nearly all older than I am or else much younger: the nicest girl on board is about three years old, and there is no one between her and her mother. Just as we left Brisbane the New Guinea boat came in and all the passengers on that boat were young. I am beginning to think that the only time I like the sea is when I am on land—that is not to say that the only time I like the land is when I am at sea.

The surrounds of Brisbane were very fine. Although I was only wearing a white drill-suit I was about boiled, but I was walking hard and did not loiter as I needed some exercise after sailing for a few days. The noise of the crickets is almost as bad at times as the haymower. The wings of the butterflies were of fine gauze with coloured spots, if it were not for the spots it would be impossible to see them.

You say that Harold longs to come out here but you do not mention coming out yourself. I'm afraid that after twelve months of this weather you would be inclined to stop here.

It must have been a pretty bad storm to loosen the foundations of the riding school. I cannot make out from your letter what you say Hance thought Countess was worth. Was it two or seven hundred pounds? I am glad to hear that the building at Moorlands is getting on a little better, Jaques really is the limit with it: in Sydney I saw four storeys of a ten-storey building go up within the space of a month.

I was surprised to hear that the Lagonda has been sheeted up, I thought you would have been using it, but I suppose it has been too wet for an open car. People over here complain that the seasons are changing for the worse and that the summers are getting rather poor: I don't know what they have to grumble about.

I had a letter from Dodie*. I wish I had been able to go to the Motor Show with them, of course, I know all about it having devoured all the motor papers I could get hold of out here. I see that the Lagonda had gone up in price now that it has got a longer guarantee. The new 80 m.p.h. model should prove a serious competitor to the Bentley as it is only half the price. I am longing to drive again, for although I have motored quite a lot I have not had the chance to drive at all. Of course, all the cars out here are American, and in spite of the fact that they suit the conditions, they do not suit me.

At the moment we are passing a rocky coast with hundreds of wooded islands; they look very fine. I am quite warm enough in an open shirt. Today I see in the news that England is pretty well ice-bound.

Well, I must close now and do a bit more scribbling to others. By the way, it is now six months since I left home and I am considering whether to spend the spare months in Japan or India. It depends whether I can rearrange my bookings.

Love from,
John.

P.S. Please ask Harold to let me know the date of the 1928 art silk exhibition.

* His sister, Dora.

THE QUEENSLAND COAST

We arrived in Cairns at about seven o'clock and found it fearfully hot. The surrounds of Cairns are very pretty but a bit inaccessible to visitors and I had little time to spare. However, I had a good walk round the town, took a few snaps, and retired to the ship to smoke and cool off a bit.

We have five new passengers on board, a Mrs. Fox with her two nieces and two nephews, a very welcome addition to our crowd. Mrs. Fox is an elderly lady but very nice and a good sport, the two boys will be about eighteen and nineteen and are quite nice chaps, Min is twenty or so but is very quiet and seems much younger, Brigette is rather like Beatrice Hindley to look at, she will be about twenty-one, quite lively and clever and a good sport, in fact we could do with half a dozen like her.

CHRISTMAS 1927

Christmas Day dawned like any other day in the tropics as we steamed towards Thursday Island. In the morning we all had a drink with the captain. At night we had a good dinner and a fancy dress dance, yours truly being "Miss Taiping", anyway I was cool. We had a good time and the two Chinese girls came up from the second class, one was about fifteen or sixteen and the other about twenty, they were both charming girls and their English was a treat to listen to, so very soft and totally unlike the Australian accent.

Boxing Day, 1927

Boxing Day saw us on Thursday Island.

Thursday Island is one of the romantic Pearling Islands about which one reads and believes. There may be "romances", but an island seven miles round and carrying a population of less than 200 whites and few thousand coloureds, including Aborigines, Latins, Japs, Malays and Chinese, does not appeal to me. The buildings, as I had suspected, are of corrugated metal: some of the slum areas are enough to make one ill. The fine coconut trees are the only thing that give the place a tropical air: apart from the trees there is no indication that one is further north than Brisbane—except that the heat is more intense, and there are more flies.

The pearling ships are luggers carrying a mixed crew with a Jap captain, they usually cruise and fish for three to four weeks at a time before returning to the island: the principal source of revenue is the pearl shell and the crocus shell, the pearls themselves are regarded more as a bonus.

The worst feature of Thursday Island is the hopeless outlook, day follows day without a change of any sort except perhaps the arrival of a ship; it must be a terrible thing for children to be brought up there.

S.S. *Taiping*
Thursday Island.
27th December, 1927

Dear Harold and Arthur,

Thanks so very much for your wire in which you say "do not hurry home" and that you can manage without me for a few more months. I am certainly trying to get all the experience I can, most people recommend seeing Japan so I shall find out about booking when I get to Hong Kong. I received your cable last week. Vernie sent me Christmas and New Year greetings by cable from Sydney which was good of him.

We are having quite a nice trip but are short of young people, most of the older ones, however, are very nice. Yesterday, of course, felt very strange being away from the children, and the absence of the usual Xmassy feeling. It was not too bad however, and at night we had a fancy dress dance, on a Sunday! Well, why not? This is Australia and not Europe.

I am very glad that we called here. If you ever get the chance, do go and see *The Hound of the Deep*, it was filmed out here.

One reads about the romantic pearling islands, but give me Blacko any day: just imagine living on an unsanitary, hot island with only about 200 other white people, and just think of the children having to be brought up in a place like that. You usually see very attractive photos of places such as this—so I went round the back streets to take mine.

Well, we are leaving the island now, so I must close.

Love to all, John.

THE "ROMANTIC PEARLING ISLAND"

Note by V. Cutter 10/4/84
Thursday Island is the navigational and administrative headquarters

of the islands of the Torres Straits, this Strait is 130km wide and runs between Cape York (Australia) and Papua. The main shipping route is known as the Prince of Wales Channel, it requires professional pilots to navigate the shoals and reefs of this coral sea.

The Torres islanders have Malayan affinity: they were later arrivals than the Aborigines, and were noted for their early ferocity and seafaring talents.

Towards the end of the nineteenth century the pearling industry was booming, and scores of luggers were based in its sheltered waters. The employees worked under appalling conditions for which the industry was notorious; the diving casualty rate was very high, and from time to time cyclonic storms caused heavy loss of life. Most of the stations at that time were owned by Europeans.

In the 1930s the Japanese perfected the cultivation of pearls by artificial means, and the pearl-diving industry greatly declined. Later the mother-of-pearl was replaced by the use of plastic in the button-making industry.

At this time steamers and warships plying between Australia and East India ports, used it as a coaling station. Fortifications were built and guns placed at the island's highest point in order to dominate the narrow reef passages which all vessels must negotiate between Australia and New Guinea. The military garrison was withdrawn from the island in 1933.

Some pearling vessels still operate from Thursday Island, and employ divers to obtain the young oysters suitable for pearl culture. The luggers are still owned and operated by the Torres Straits Islanders, although the cultured pearl farms in nearby waters are mainly run by the Australians and Japanese in partnership.

INTRODUCTION

The Far East

MANILA — HONG KONG — SHANGHAI — HONG KONG —
SINGAPORE — PENANG — CEYLON (SRI LANKA)

V. Cutter
10/4/84

★   ★   ★

Manila had been an American possession since the turn of the century, but at the time of John Hindley's visit they were only just starting to use English as the official language in government affairs and in education. Large amounts of money were being spent by the Americans on capital projects and on education: the mile-long barracks was the showplace of the American army. John Hindley's remark about the natives "seeming to think that they can run the place themselves" is spoken like a true young imperialist, but it was nevertheless perceptive.

The population of Hong Kong would have been only a fraction of that of present times—due to vast immigration and increase in the birth rate: it is hard to imagine that in 1927 the major building would be only a few storeys high.

In Shanghai, the place where John Hindley sounds to have been having such a good time would have been in the International Settlement. In Viki Baum's book *Nanking Road*★ she says, "The Shanghai Hotel stands half-way between the English racecourse and the Bund. . . it was bombed in 1937—up till then it was considered that the International Settlement in Shanghai was inviolable." Of the Chinese

★Reference 2—see page 156

Troubles she says, "In 1927 the British government decided to support Chiang Kai-shek against the menace of the Japanese, as well as against the spread of communism in China. Up to now China had been treated without compunction, like a colony: now officials were required who had some slight understanding of the country and its tortuous psychology, and who were liked by the Chinese."

Singapore was under the administration of the British by 1928, and it was already a very important port for world shipping.

★ ★ ★

TO MANILA

S.S. Taiping.

After leaving Thursday Island we failed to see land for two days. Then we passed Bird Island which is an extinct volcano miles from anywhere. It is covered with birds and snakes—how the latter have got there is unknown. We sailed in amongst many small islands and soon we were passing the north-east corner of the Celebes; it was very interesting as any sort of transport within the islands is obviously very difficult except by water. From Celebes onwards we were passing islands continuously and it was fascinating to study the currents and the stuff they carry along.

On Tuesday evening we passed Zarangani, as we were very close inshore it was possible to get a fair idea of the native villages and to see the huts which were mostly made of bamboo and were built on poles. The town is the port of a very big cocoa plantation.

We saw many native craft of various descriptions, mostly with very light hulls provided with outriggers and carrying an enormous spread of canvas.

MANILA

We arrived at about nine o'clock, and by 10.00 a.m. I had hired a car and set off for a couple of hours of sight seeing. The houses are for the most part very nice, the hotels also, though, of course, they are very tropical in style. The foliage as one would expect was vivid with many creepers and climbers.

The natives are not a nice crowd. Lately they have been causing trouble, as they imagine that they can run the place themselves. As labourers they are good workers and poorly paid, they also do most of the semi-skilled work and are policemen, drivers and shopkeepers. In appearance, if it were not for their colouring, they look very like Americans—in fact it would be very difficult to tell the difference as they all tend to wear peaked caps and glasses.

The harbour is about thirty miles long and about twenty miles wide. The harbour entrance is about five miles wide and in the middle is a splendid fort known as the "Gibraltar of the East". The reason for its importance is that the harbour and the bay provide anchorage and a base for the American Navy in the East; it has a wonderful position and should be able to guard against anything. Only a small American force is at present in occupation, the rest is away cruising. There is no doubt that it is a wonderful base, but it appears to me to be unnecessarily large for the size of American possession of territory in the East.

We visited the prison, I was very disgusted, not with the prison itself, but with the Americans. Every day the prisoners are drilled at 4.30 p.m. to music and old sentimental songs played by a band dressed as the Foreign Legion (but not as smartly). A squad dressed in uniform and carrying dummy rifles then go through a bit of platoon drill. A more disgusting exhibition of rank bad discipline it is impossible to imagine, any British O.T.C. platoon could gain them points.

The dress of the local women is various, but the chief unusual item is the large sleeves which are heavily starched and are about eight inches long and ten inches in diameter.

The rule of the road is supposed to be to keep left.

At night we went to St. Anna and arrived back here about 1.30 p.m. I went to bed at 4.00 p.m. and between times—well, least said soonest mended.

S.S. *Taiping*
Manila to Hong Kong.
5th January, 1928

Dear Reg,

We are just catching the north-east monsoon and although the sea is not too bad and the ship is behaving splendidly most of the passengers are still in bed—or at any rate they are very quiet and thoughtful.

I had a very late night on Tuesday, slept yesterday afternoon and consequently couldn't sleep last night. I got up at 5.30 this morning to do a little packing as we expect to be in Hong Kong by tomorrow: it is now only 10.00 a.m. but I am ready to sit down and take a rest and write, as all the time I have not been eating I have been walking. I enclose some snaps which I took with my new camera.

We have had a very good trip altogether, especially the last week or so. Two girls about my own age came on board at Cairns, both good sports and quite good dancers, they have certainly bucked things up a bit; previously we had only a few pieces of mutton! Some dressed as lamb and others not, which reminds me—.

About the Townsville Show. At Townsville we saw some motor-cycle races; and a stockman who cracked whips, he was so big and heavy that he could hardly get out of the way of the thong; and last and best we saw some goat races. The goats were just ordinary ones and were harnessed to small trotting carts driven by boys, the race was about a quarter of a mile and was really quite exciting—even if it was a bit slow.

A few of us bathed at Townsville. I am not making much progress, if I dive in I get along quite well, but by just falling in I cannot get going.

At Thursday Island a few of us bathed again, the baths were rotten and the water was dirty, all the same it seemed quite nice with the beautiful sun until the following day when we began to feel the burns. Thursday Island is one of the series of pearling stations; we saw most of the ships and some shells, but no pearls.

We had a good time at Manila but I would not like to live there: in mid-winter we were having lunch out in the open with only a roof over us, and even with sun blinds we were boiled. Manila is the American naval base in the East. What puzzles me is why does America need such a large force out here?

In Manila five of us had a drive round the town both in the morning and in the afternoon, and at night five of us went out to dance. We had a splendid time, with a good band and an even better floor, such a change after the ship. To bed at about 4.00 a.m. and the ship left Manila for Hong Kong at 6.00 a.m.

I am not going to finish up with a lecture, but whilst you are at school do pay plenty of attention to your history and to geography, and also to the imports and exports of various countries. If you have lessons about the wind and weather, which I'm sure you will, it will pay you well to remember all you can. I now realize that things which I thought to be so unimportant at school, and which I did not take as much interest in as I should have done, would make a tremendous difference to my travelling: things which people point out to me now, I really should be able to have found out for myself.

Well, I must close now, we are running a few hours late for Hong Kong, so it will be midday tomorrow when we arrive. I believe that it is very interesting and strange. From there I go to Shanghai and to as many other places as possible in the time.

I expect I shall be home before Gisburn races.

Cheerio,
John.

HONG KONG

6th January, 1928

We sighted Hong Kong at first light and by ten in the morning we had got amongst all the junks, etc. Although they look terribly clumsy they are very fast and can be handled in a remarkable manner. One man was sculling a punt in a sea that was making the *Taiping* roll considerably.

The coast of Hong Kong is extremely barren and very rugged, but the sea at the entrance to the harbour is quite calm and does not seem to be affected by the tide very much. The winds across the harbour are pretty strong, and I certainly felt cold for a time, soon, however, I felt all right and the refreshing wind has made me feel better now than I have done for weeks.

The streets of Hong Kong are very fascinating with all the Chinese about, their dress consists of a coat and trousers, or the long "priest's" coat with a black felt hat. The majority of the people are clean, but the beggars are filthy and are terribly scarred with disease. Many Chinese wear sabots, and their clip-clop, clip-clop reminds me of the sound of the clogs at home—only the sound is not loud enough.

The women for the most part wear long cloaks and no hat, and many of them, as do the men, lean forward with their arms folded and trot along in a slouching manner at a pace of about five miles per hour. The better-class women wear European, or semi-European clothes: although many of them, especially those of the highest rank will not mix with Europeans, and adopt neither their customs nor their clothes.

The Hong Kong dollar must be the most filthy coin in the world.

One of the most interesting places is the waterfront, here one sees porters carrying all sorts of things on their bamboo poles; others are pulling great cumbersome two-wheeled wagons which look like ox-wagons.

The better-class Chinese and most of the Europeans ride in the semi-sedan chair which the coolies carry on their shoulders, otherwise they ride in rickshaws pulled by one man and sometimes pushed by two more. The women are to be seen carrying loads equal to that of the men, they do all the men's jobs except for carrying the sedan chairs and the rickshaw work.

The Hotel Hong Kong costs ten dollars per day for bed and breakfast, dinner is one dollar downstairs or two dollars fifty in the grill-room: there is dancing in the grill-room during dinner. The rooms are light and airy, but the bedrooms are without bathrooms. There are lounges and writing-rooms on the ground and first floors. The service is quite good, but boys who ask for tips do not get any.

There were plenty of silk goods in the shop opposite the hotel, also at Pioneers in Queen Street. The Repulse Bay was well worth a visit, but I did not see inside the rooms. The Peak Hotel was smothered in mist, and will be so for days on end—the best months to stay there are in January, February or March.

> Hong Kong Hotel,
> Hong Kong.
> 7th January, 1928

Dear Harold and Gertrude,

We arrived here yesterday after a very calm, fine, cool and generally pleasant trip. I have not had time to see much of Hong Kong, nor will I have, as I go to Shanghai on Tuesday, and will only have one other day here on the return journey.

If I don't go to Shanghai on Tuesday I cannot get a fast ship. To go to Japan I would have to go straight on from Shanghai, and even then I would only get two days in Japan, so I have decided to cut it out. I would like to have seen Japan, but may as well leave something for the next trip.

There is no B.D.A. representative out here in Hong Kong so I thought I would go up to Shanghai as soon as possible, and will have about eight days there.

Most of the *Taiping* passengers are staying at this hotel so I hardly feel to have left the ship. Most of the people are old, but a few of us have had a very good time and I should not mind going back to Sydney on this ship—but I must go on to Malaya and catch the S.S. *Antenor* at Penang for India.

This place is very strange, but I am beginning to get accustomed to strange things and don't break my neck every time anything unusual passes by.

Well, I will write when I have more time next week on the ship, if I remember.

Love from,
John.

SHANGHAI

19th January

I bought no Chinese silks or anything in Shanghai owing to the excessive prices. The shops of note are in Yates Road which is some distance from the Bund.

The Majestic Hotel is quite nice, but far too expensive forty-five dollars per double room and single twenty-five to thirty dollars, food included. It is probably worth a visit for a tea-dance or dinner dancing, but the food is reputedly not too good.

The Palace Hotel is twenty-four dollars per double room and fifteen dollars per single room, all in. All the bedrooms have a bathroom and also a writing-desk. A bed-sitting-room is forty-five dollars. The rooms are plain and simple but clean, and the food in the Grill-room is some of the best I have tasted since leaving home.

Places to go:-

Astor House for tea-dances 5.00 - 7.00 p.m.

The French Club for tea-dancing 5.00 - 8.00 p.m. three times weekly (an introduction is necessary).

The Plaza, the Little Club, and The Plantation are all worth visiting after 11.00 p.m.

The Tavern after midnight.

The Palace Hotel,
Shanghai.
20th January, 1928

Dear Harold and Gertrude,

I am having an excellent time here and don't want to leave, but as I have my passage booked, and it will be seven months tomorrow since I left, I had better face homewards.

Three of the *Taiping* passengers, a boy and girl of about my own age and their aunt, came up to from Hong Kong with me as they have some friends in Shanghai. We have had a very good time here together.

We spent Friday looking round the town until about 5.00 p.m. when we went to a tea-dance until 8.00 p.m.; we then dined, and went off again about 10.00 p.m. to dance. On Saturday we did the same, except that we finished up at a cabaret at 3.00 a.m. on Sunday morning. Sunday was a quiet day and we only danced from 5.00 p.m. to 8.00 p.m. On Monday we repeated Friday's outing but at different places.

The others left for Singapore on Tuesday; it was just as well as it enabled me to get a bit of sleep. It was rather a pity that we could not have sailed together, but they had to return to Australia and could not wait for me. I thought I ought to stay here a few more days and justify my existence in ways other than dancing.

To get to the more serious side, I do not yet require the money which I wired for, so have arranged for a letter of credit at the bank. If I had waited until I really needed it it may have delayed me waiting for the cable, and I did not want to miss the boat at one of the Indian ports. I have made no arrangements as to how to get there from Singapore, but will see what Preston of B.D.A. has to suggest.

I have met Simpson out here, he has been very good to me and taken me out and introduced me to people: he has also made me a member of the Shanghai Club (which incidentally has the longest straight bar in the world). Simpson has also sent his man round the shops with me to buy patterns.

I have tried to match these patterns up with our own pattern, without much success. The big business that is done out here is in black satins and in real silks. The enclosed patterns will give you some idea of the cloths, the countries of origin, and the prices which are really painful!

The prices I have quoted are per piece. (I thought I had better mention it in case you thought they were expensive per yard.)

The best quality art silk out here is manufactured in Italy, but it seems likely that the art silk trade out here will be killed altogether by the increases in duty. There is already a 10% duty on all wines and spirits; next week there is to be a 2½% tax on all luxury goods, 5% for customs and 20% for the National Government; there is fear of this duty being extended to many other goods including art silk.

I am glad to see that at home the employees and employers are at last holding a conference to suggest ways of reducing the costs of production. They have certainly got their work cut out and I hope some good comes of it. But surely the employers never expected the workers to agree to any wage cut or extension of working hours?

The other day I had a good look at the customs figures. The way that Japan is getting or rather, has already got hold of the market out here is terrible; every year she gets a bigger and bigger share. The trouble is that she can land coloured goods cheaper than we can import grey cloth, and as she is only thirty-six hours sailing away, anything new that comes into the market here is immediately copied by Japan at a lower price.

The samples of ours that I mention below have been immensely admired especially the latter two, but the price would kill them out here. It is rather a bad time to be calling at the shops as the Chinese New Year starts at the week-end, and they have a week's holiday. They also settle their accounts at this time and much of the stuff sold in the shops is old and cheap as the shopkeepers try to get their money in so that they can settle up their own accounts. However, I think that the samples that I have got are fairly good. Chung, the man who went round with me, seemed to know his job.

Well, I must close now, I hope you are keeping well and enjoying some good hunting. I saw a picture of the opening meet at Gisburn in a Bradford paper and thought I saw you but I am not certain.

Love from,
John.

Blue Funnel Line   T.S.S. *Antenor,*
Hong Kong.
25th January, 1928

Dear Harold,

I have just received a big batch of letters intended to reach me before Christmas, which by the way, is held on 25th December not January 25th both here and in Australia!

You seem to be having a sticky time of it at home with the orders dropping off and the silk going all wrong. I was very suprised to hear that you are having trouble with the Brysilka, I had hoped that by now you would have got over all that. By the way, Simpson and two of his friends were talking about it the other day and asking what was the cause—so I told them just as much as was good for them. Of course, Simpson thought it was the fault of the manufacturers, and I had to think it was the dyers. I hope you will soon get to the bottom of the barré* trouble and settle it for good, it seems such a shame that a cloth

---

* Threads being uneven in the finished fabric.

like that should be handicapped by production and this other trouble, it is certainly very much admired everywhere.

We had a very bad trip down here, it was all right once we got going, but we ran aground within two hours of leaving Shanghai and then the fog got worse. We had to anchor for about twenty-four hours so that we had only covered seventy-one miles in the first forty-eight hours of the journey. After that we came down at a great pace and did 399 miles in twenty-four hours but it was too late to catch up all we had lost so we did not get ashore until 11.00 a.m. I was too late to see Watson here, he left Hong Kong at 12 noon. I could have just about seen him, but knowing what it is like getting people away from you when you are sailing, I thought he would be more pleased not to see me.

The sea was calm and the weather fairly warm, so we were pretty comfortable but very quiet, they say the ship usually livens up at Singapore or Colombo. I met one of my Australian friends in Shanghai, he is an engineer on one of the coastal ships and I was fortunate enough to be able to find him there on board. I also met two Americans who had come up to Shanghai with us, I just happened to see them passing the hotel window here. I had hoped that they were also going to Colombo later on, but they have decided not to go.

We have only picked up a few more passengers at Hong Kong, they do not have the appearance of being very bright. It is rather surprising that out of a crowd of about forty passengers we have at least four who are going round the world. At present there are very few people travelling anywhere except coming home on leave. Everyone I met says that the Pacific ships are practically empty, and I know that the ships on the other runs are with the possible exception of the Atlantic.

I am probably going to have some difficulty in getting from Singapore or Penang to Rangoon. I would like to go to India by train from Penang but there is a fifty mile stretch without rail, which is most annoying. The only way to get overland to Rangoon is to walk or to travel by mule, but that is over the mountains and I don't think that I shall go that way.

The house does not seem to be progressing very favourably, I hope you are well settled in by the time you get this letter.

I am glad to hear that George has turned out so well this season but it's a pity that you are not getting more hunting. It seems such a waste of good weather for me to be spending it at sea when I might be using the same weather at home in a much better manner. I can still remember every wet day that I have had since leaving home—and they are only just into double figures.

Jack Hance sounds to be very pleased with Countess. I was rather surprised at the price he put on her, Gertrude had told me about it before, but I thought her seven was supposed to be a two.

I hope you are all keeping well at home, and are getting some better weather.

Love to all,
John.

T.S.S. *Antenor*
Singapore.
29th January, 1928

Dear Harold and Gertrude,

I was very glad to get a bunch of letters this morning which had been posted on about 6th Jan. It was quite a change to get some recent news, and not to have to wait five or six weeks.

Trade sounds to be very bad at home at present, and I really cannot see it getting much help by trading with the East unless prices can be reduced. Costs can only be cut by an alteration in taxation or a reduction in wages: With regard to the former, the money has to be found somewhere, of course, and I should imagine that there is more scope for saving in the unemployment money than elsewhere.

People sit at home and grumble about the cost of the maintainance of the army and the navy, especially at places such as this, but I can now understand why we need such an enormous fleet. It looks to me that Singapore will some day be of as much importance, if not more, to us as is Gibraltar. A fleet which is stationed here can keep an eye on Australia, China and India, which are all too far from England and too near to America and Japan, to be left unprotected (especially from Japan who would like to get Australia for herself).

When people talk about the so called "waste of money" in sending troops out to China they want to discuss it with someone who was there during The Troubles. The troops here are not usually needed to fight, but a British regiment or the presence of a battleship has the same moral effect in the East as armoured cars, etc., had during the strike at home. I can assure you, it was very nice to be able to look out of my window in the morning and see the H.M.S. *Vindictive* lying in Shanghai harbour.

To get back to production costs—Vol. 1, part 2! Wages are very difficult to compare in different countries as there is no doubt that the climate (which is not usually taken into account when comparing the cost of living) plays a very important part. After seeing Australia I am dead against the reduction of wages of any sort in England except as absolutely the last resort.

I would admit that the wages in Australia are altogether far too high, but there is no doubt that although their trades are supposed to be taxed out of existence, most people seem to thrive off it.

I hope to see the difficulties of Lancashire overcome without any increase in hours or reduction of wages, but it is apparently going to prove to be a very difficult task, for, in spite of one of the big bankers saying a couple of days ago in London that, "the demand for art silk far exceeds the present supply and is likely to do so for a long time," it seems to me that the trouble in Lancashire is *over-production*, especially of cotton, which the foreigner can produce almost as well and at a far lower cost.

After reading through that little effort I find that I have not yet repeated myself so had better change the subject before I do. It is difficult to try carrying on a discussion by post when you have to wait a couple of months for an answer, but I may as well keep my hand in.

To get back to Singapore, I have only been here a couple of hours, and as it is Sunday I am having a pretty slack time of it all day. I would not have written tonight but I wanted to answer your letters before leaving as I don't know how the post will be over the next few weeks.

I shall certainly go to Penang from here by rail on either Tuesday or Wednesday, and I shall almost certainly have to take a ship from there to get to Colombo, then work back to Calcutta from there. I am sorry that I cannot go all the way by rail, but there isn't any in parts of Burma, and I must go by the route which allows me to see the most in the least amount of time.

I was rather surprised to hear that Reg has a tutor, but I think he won't regret it later and I shall be able to add a little pidgin English to his languages. The best bit I have heard so far was when someone asked a coolie what a big tin-covered barge on the river was for. He said, "That belong to topside walkee man." I'll send you an interpretation later on!

I'm glad to hear that Reg can now make a fire, make tea, and also carve; I shall see that he doesn't forget when I get back. Well, I don't think I have any more to tell you, as I seem to have written yards in the last few days I will finish now.

Love from,

John.

T.S.S. *Antenor,*

Post card to—Master R. Hindley,

Arnside, Westmorland,

England.

Dear Reg,

I am on the way from Hong Kong to Singapore, the weather is good and the sea calm, but the ship is rather dull.

The *Antenor* is rather like the ship on this postcard.

Cheerio,

John.

MALAYA

THE STRAITS SETTLEMENTS

SINGAPORE

Arrived in Singapore on Sunday, 25th January and left early on Wednesday. I went to Penang by train and caught the S.S. *Antenor* there. I saw nothing of the proposed naval base at Singapore, but I am very glad that I called there.

The city very much resembles other Eastern cities where there is a mixture of native and European buildings, but all the time the former are giving way to the latter.

The usual sights are to be seen, fruit vendors sitting on the pavements selling anything from orange peel upwards. The beggars are almost as filthy as those of Hong Kong. The porters carry loads that would slow a horse considerably; the itinerate fruit and chow-man (how I long to sample his mixtures), carpenters, plumbers, etc., all carrying their total belongings at one end, and their wares at the other end of a bamboo pole. The poultry man with his queer beehive shaped basket of poultry together with a balance which consists of a beam suspended in the middle with a hook at one end and a sliding weight at the other. Bullock carts are in abundance, and some of the animals are very fine, but one never by any chance sees a horse.

All the clerks appear to be Chinese as they are considered to be honest and to have a head for figures. Many streets have open drains which I was rather disquieted to see; I should have thought a British Possession to be above that.

The Chinese do most of the cargo handling and the portering, they are also the rickshaw boys as they are the only race capable of standing up to the strain. Many of the native quarters in Singapore are as Chinese as those in Shanghai, with the possible exception that they may be a bit cleaner and the streets a bit wider.

The country around Singapore is very pretty although I should tire of the palms after a time, everything is such a wonderful green. The houses are very beautiful from the outside but I did not see the interior of any. One hears of the smell of rubber and copra but I hardly noticed it, and the flies did not bother me at all.

There are many thousands of Chinese in Malaya, and also dozens of other races who do all the work—the Malayan being too dignified and lazy to work. He likes to become a policeman or a soldier, to wear a uniform or to carry a gun or baton, but hard work, no! The soil is exceptionally fertile and the sea abounds with fish, so if living in the country he can satisfy his simple requirements by one day's work a week.

SINGAPORE TO PENANG

I left Singapore at about 7.30 for Penang, the countryside was very interesting and for the most part wooded. The train passes through thousands of acres of rubber trees, there are also lots of pineapple, pawpaw, bananas and coconut trees, although the latter appear to be grown more by the individual villager rather than on the larger estates.

It is surprising what a fascination the railway has for the Oriental—hundreds of natives, in fact I should imagine practically the entire village, collects on the station whenever a train comes in. All colours are to be seen but almost half of them are Chinese with their inevitable umbrellas.

The trains are fairly comfortable, being metre-gauge with seating on only one side of the passage. The food was very poor. The sleepers were two-berth and were both roomy and moderately comfortable, but of course, the whole train gets filthy with having to have the windows wide open.

Prai station is the terminal station and at one time it was the proposed harbour. Owing to a lack of foresight, an enormous amount of money spent on the harbour works only to find that the silt which built up would not allow the big ships to enter, also that the river was too narrow for much shipping.

The island of Penang will be about fifty miles round. It is unlike Hong Kong in that it has a lot of low-lying and level ground, and that the mountain peaks that it possesses are always cool and clear. Coconut palms can be seen by the thousand and they, and the native huts, make a very pretty scene, especially if one can also catch a glimpse of the ocean. Palatines and many strange palms grow profusely, as does rubber and pineapple. The residences appear to be very desirable places with fine gardens attached.

The people here are practically the same as in Singapore, i.e. very mixed. The port I consider to be a great help, for although it takes a lot of the Singapore trade it does mean a saving of freight from the west, and what is more important, it forms a second line of defence (although I believe that Penang is at present unarmed).

Which reminds me that I have now found out why the British wanted six inch guns instead of the American eight inch gun. Britain could in the event of war, have a very formidable fleet of armed merchantmen, whereas the American merchant ships cannot be armed as the thrust of an eight inch gun throws too great a strain on a merchant ship.

T.S.S. *Antenor*
Penang to Colombo.
5th February, 1928

Dear Reg,

We are carrying mail on this ship so it has not been worth posting this letter previously. Please would you make sure your father gets the enclosed, it is just a note of my plans and a forwarding address for him.

I had a most interesting run from Singapore to Penang. It was hot of course, and very dirty, but one gets accustomed to that when travelling by rail. I was thinking as I went what a difference between travelling in the L.Y.R. with the windows down and the steam on, and the Malayan railways where you have a window with a fly-shield and sunscreen. I didn't use either of these and consequently got absolutely filthy. The only clothes necessary are a shirt and shorts, preferably in khaki.

The country would be best described as fascinating rather than beautiful, although some stretches are wonderful. The railway runs right through the jungle which comes to within yards of the line in most places but, because it is so dense, one cannot see more than a couple of yards into it nor can one see the forest floor beyond the first ten feet or so.

The rubber plantations are not very interesting after you have seen the first one: there is nothing to see except thousands of trees with the bark cut, and with a small cup attached to catch the rubber as it falls. Tin mining is the greatest source of wealth after rubber. I was very surprised to find that 50% of all the world's rubber and tin come from Malaya.

Like almost all parts of the East, Malaya is filled with Chinese, who work very much better than the natives who are a very lazy lot: they don't mind being policemen or soldiers, but object to work.

The Malayans do not appear to be a downtrodden race like the South African natives, but seem to be quite contented, as long as they can lie about in the sun, do a bit of gardening, and fish occasionally. They only seem to work about one day a week.

Penang is a very beautiful island, and I wish I could have stayed for a few days, I took some photos that ought to be very interesting if they come out, which they should as the light was good.

We have a very nice crowd on board now, but as I shall be leaving it tomorrow at Colombo, I will have to find my feet on a new ship for the homeward journey.

Well, I have no more news now, but you will be hearing from me pretty often when I am in India.

Cherrio,
John.

T.S.S. Antenor
Penang to Colombo.
5th February, 1928

Dear Harold,

I am just waiting to hear from Thomas Cook when I get to Colombo regarding my itinerary, I have made enquiries as to travelling through India by rail, I shall definitely be able to see Bombay, Delhi, Calcutta and Madras. The train journey will last about three weeks and will cost appoximately £40, but the full month from leaving the *Antenor* at

Colombo now to catching the *Hector* home from Colombo in March, will cost over £100 as I shall be stopping off in India at a few places of special interest.

Yours,
John.

P.S. Next letters to T.S.S *Hector* ·
   Consortium Savon Freres,
      Blue Funnel Agents,
         Marseilles.
P.P.S. Port about 18th March.

CEYLON

6th February, 1928

We arrived in Colombo Harbour early on 6th February. I had got clear of the customs and had arranged a room by 9.30 a.m. I wrote a batch of postcards and spent the morning walking round. I took a couple of photos of bullock carts and the like. The bullocks by the way, are much smaller than the ones in Singapore, and two of them are usually used for the bigger types of cart.

In the afternoon we visited the fruit market, a typical oriental place, so I took a couple of photos there. I saw some cucumbers at least five feet long. A man was practically sitting in a trough washing fruit, whilst someone else was washing a child in the same water.

I am staying at the Great Oriental Hotel, it is the most convenient place, although many prefer the Galle Face. The tariff is fifteen rupees for a single room, all in. Tip the baggage boys at the time, as they are coolies. It is advisable to tip the bedroom boy and let him tip the bedroom coolies.

I am just off to Mont Lavinia and to the native city, I also want to see the gardens; the trip for four or five people by taxi will cost twenty rupees. The Thomas Cook office is just next to the hotel so I shall call there tomorrow. I have been told not to rely on them for booking berths, etc., also warned against buying things in the stores here.

7th February

I have spent the day looking in curio shops, and getting stung buying a few odds and ends and needs, such as pyjamas. I have also been arranging my tour through India for which I need bedding, which will cost me about £4 10s 0d. I also have to get a bearer and at present have two in view.

Now that I sit down and think about it I wonder if it is worthwhile. If I spend the month here in Ceylon, or anywhere else, it would cost me about £60 to £70, whereas the tour of India will cost at least £100, and I doubt whether I shall have time to see much, as twelve out of the nineteen days will be spent in the train. There are only a few short stops, namely Bombay, Madras, Agra, Lucknow and Calcutta. The longer I think about it the more I dislike the idea of the journey, then, to put the lid on it, I can hear the crows cawing and they make me long terribly to get home.

My views about travelling alone have undergone a complete change. On board a ship it is all right, in fact it is often an advantage with ports such as Hong Kong and Singapore; but travelling alone—there is nothing to be said for it except that it makes you think for yourself.

8th February

I had a quiet day and fixed up my ticket and a bearer. As I have decided to leave with de Meyeda, I left hurriedly today.

INTRODUCTION

India

MADRAS — BOMBAY — AGRA — DELHI — CALCUTTA

A railway journey through India taking a round trip from the
south over a period of three weeks.

V. Cutter
10/4/84

★ ★ ★

There is little need for explanation of this last episode of the diary,
which is a straightforward train journey, except perhaps to consider the
abrupt end to the writing.

There was no intention of John Hindley doing any business in India,
or of seeing anything of the textile industry, except a visit to a mill in
Delhi, which was by accident. Yet it was from this very country that the
competition to the cotton manufacturers in Lancashire was to come, in
increasing severity, in the years ahead.

The diary ends abruptly in Delhi, about one week before he was due
to retrace the route back to Ceylon from Madras. It is known that John
Hindley returned home via the Suez Canal, but no letters, photos, press
cuttings, menus or passengers lists, which he had collected so
assiduously throughout the trip remain of India or thereafter.

Perhaps a diary is lost, but it is more likely that John Hindley, like
many other European travellers in India, was so saturated by the sights,
sounds and smells of the country, not to mention the myriads of people,
that he could absorb and write no more.

Thos. COOK & Son Ltd.
Colombo.
J. Hindley, Esq.

10th Feb. 1928	Dep.	Colombo Fort	19.00 hrs.
11th	Arr.	Talaimannar Pier	6.00
11th	Dep.	do.	7.20
11th	Arr.	Dhanushkodi Pier	9.30
11th	Dep.	do.	10.40
12th	Arr.	Madura Junction	15.35
12th	Dep.	do.	15.50
13th	Arr.	Madras. Egmore	7.00
13th	Dep.	do.	21.05
15th	Arr.	Bombay. Victoria	6.45
17th	Dep.	do.	13.15
18th	Arr.	Agra. Cant.	16.10
20th	Dep.	do.	16.25
20th	Arr.	Delhi. Main	20.05
22nd	Dep.	do.	18.35
22nd	Arr.	Morabad	23.46
23rd	Dep.	do.	.02
24th	Arr.	Lucknow	7.00
24th	Dep.	do.	10.45
25th	Arr.	Benares	15.37
25th	Dep.	do.	15.45
26th	Arr.	Calcutta	7.30
27th	Dep.	do.	17.06
	Ret.		
29th	Arr.	Madras. Central	8.00
29th	Dep.	Madras. Egmore	20.40
1st Mar. 1928	Arr.	Dhanushkodi Pier	16.15
1st	Dep.	do.	17.10
1st	Arr.	Talaimannar Pier	19.20
1st	Dep.	do.	20.15
2nd	Arr.	Colombo Fort	8.15

Thos. COOK & Son Ltd.,   Post Box No. 36
Passage Department.   Colombo.
Telegraphic address "Coupon".   7th February, 1928
To:—
   J. Hindley, Esq., Room No. 402,
   Grand Oriental Hotel, Colombo.
Dear Sir,
   With reference to our conversation, we enclose herewith itinerary starting from Colombo on the 10th instant, and returning to Colombo. To include Madras, Bombay, Calcutta, etc.
   Bedding can be hired at the rate of Rs 1/- for each passenger. A deposit of Rs 60/- should be left with us and kept until such time as the bedding is returned to us.
   The bearer Ryan is a travelling servant and is known to us. The usual terms for bearers are as follows:-

                Wage Rs 3/- per day.
                The third class rail ticket for the trip.
                An allowance of Rs 15/- for warm clothes.

   The servant should be sent back to Colombo from any place you discharge him.

Enclosure   Yours faithfully,
  HR/AJ   pro Thos. COOK & Son Ltd.

CEYLON TO INDIA

February 1928

   We left Colombo Fort at 6.00 p.m. just as a storm was breaking with wonderful cloud effects all around. Rain started and the lightning was very vivid, but there was no thunder: the storm cleared later and we had a wonderful moonlight run. The countryside is awfully fascinating with the tremendous variety of tropical foliage. A hut surrounded by banana and a few other trees, with the moon showing round a cloud behind it is a scene I am not likely to forget. For about an hour we were able to see a comet, but then it became overcast. For the first time I saw fireflies—or they may have been fairies—they looked very pretty. I was quite disappointed when I became too tired to stay awake.
   Ceylon is a country that must be seen by day to appreciate its beauty, and I rather regret that I am not spending the month touring Ceylon, but I expect I should tire of it.

I am still doubtful about the wisdom of going as far as Delhi, it is a shame not to, yet it seems a waste of money to do so.

INDIA

9th February

We were turned out of the train at six o'clock in the morning at Talaimannar, and caught the ferry crossing over to India. I was so tired that I fell asleep on the ferry.

My first impression of India was a stretch of white sand with a few European sheds and some native huts. There was the pier with a ferry steamer moored along side; far to the right were a couple of fishing ships; about half a dozen straggley palmy-looking trees completed the unexciting picture.

The sea at this point must be practically tideless as the huts and sheds were not more than a few feet above the water. A few children swam alongside the pier to dive for money, etc.

We caught the train at Dhanushkodi and it left at about 10.40 a.m. For the first few miles the train ran alongside the sea, and in many parts only about three feet above it. All over, the land was indented with shallow bays which were some acres across but only ankle deep. There were only a few bushes and trees to be seen and occasionally we passed a man fishing; also a few gangs of plate layers who all stand to attention as the train passes, nearly every gang had a few umbrellas.

After about forty miles of passing some cultivated sand, during which time we passed over the swing bridge joining Dhanuskhoodi to the mainland, we came to more fertile country. Although it was still very sandy it seemed to hold a remarkable amount of water; rice was to be seen growing in small fields which were about thirty to forty yards square and were divided by mud walls to retain the moisture.

The number of coconuts increased as we worked northwards, and many other sorts of palms were to be seen, the names of which I do not know, but I would call them a cactus palm. It resembles an enormous stick of asparagus about a foot long and growing out of a cactus-like plant. Another, I believe, was a castor oil plant, which is more like a pawpaw than a palm. The prickly pear is to be seen growing in abundance everywhere, it is rather curious to note that the yellow and orange flowers grow on the same tree. I smelt jasmine, only a whiff, but I shall not forget it.

I saw all, or at any rate many, of the well known sights of the East.

The usual natives were mixed horribly, some fairly good looking, others not, some repulsive; many, such as the beggars, were the most loathsome creatures imaginable.

Some natives were beating rice to thresh it, and oxen were then treading it. They then grind it by means of some large wheel in a circular channel or by a large pestle in a crucible which are revolved by the oxen. The swing-bucket by the well, and the ordinary rope and chain well are to be seen everywhere, also the irrigation well. At the irrigation well, the heavy bucket is drawn up by oxen; these oxen spend their lives going backwards up an incline and then forwards down it again, if they are lucky it is a covered one to protect the driver from the sun.

I saw dozens of pigs of some strange sort, also large goats with small horns which I took to be kine. Hundreds of Indian cattle are to be seen under the charge of one man, or two or three children are guarding about a hundred. There were thousands of bullock wagons about, some with one and some with two animals pulling them.

The gleaners who have been working in the paddy-fields are beginning to return home with enormous bundles on their backs. I caught a glimpse of the fires being lit in two of the villages, and of the oxen who had finished their work being tied up for the night.

The first temple that we saw was about a quarter of a mile from the railway, and surrounded by about a hundred yards of water which was ankle deep, and in which people milled about. I saw many more temples during the course of the day, some were simple affairs of stone; some were half stone, half wood; others with figures of horses around them, but these seem to have been discarded. The first temples that I had seen seemed to be built away from the houses, but later on we saw them—elaborate but dirty—amongst the filthiest of hovels.

I took a few photos at one or two of the stations, but the train was too uncomfortable and was rocking too much to be able to take photos at any speed. At Madura Bridge station I took hundreds of natives talking, washing themselves and bathing the bullocks altogether. Near Madura I also saw a sight never to be forgotten: a group of men were looking after some kine and only about forty yards away a party of monkeys were playing and not taking the slightest notice of the men. At Kodarhanal station I took a photo of the monkey that sat on the carriage roof and then came down and took food out of your hand.

The first hills which we came across were near Madura; they were a welcome change after the flat plains. We did not, however, climb more than a few hundred feet, and we were soon away from the hills after passing the Trichinopoly Range.

The sunsets were wonderful, the Blue Mountains of Australia could not touch them for actual blue and not just a blue haze in the foreground. I saw one hill with a wonderful pair of purple peaks, they were not high, possibly about 3,000 ft., but absolute twins. There are many curious rocks scattered about, they look like huge boulders left behind by some bygone river, and are usually perfectly smooth to all appearances. Some are big enough to support large temples or a small village—there is a well known one at Trichinopoly where temples are not only built on these rocks but carved out of the sides as well. There is a famous temple at Madura but the train only stops for twenty minutes there.

MADRAS

At 10.00 a.m. I went to Binney's only to find that John Ash had gone back home. I wandered about the town for a bit and cabled for the money to be sent to Delhi. I then came back and wrote some letters and the diary, slept for a couple of hours, and later went for a motor run.

At the aquarium I saw a wonderful variety of fish of all shapes, sizes and colours. There were flat round ones, flat square ones, flat oblong ones and flat round ones with fancy fins, square globular ones and snake-shaped ones. Some were red with blue spots, some red and white, some red and black. There were striped ones, some black with yellow, having yellow tails and fins; others were red with blue stripes and brown with blue stripes. Such fish that can attach their heads to the rock and stand upright, sting-ray and catfish. Some of the fish looked like grayling but they were brown and white with a lot of frilly fins. Something called a "climbing fish" were yellow and had two pairs of underfins which were like feet. Also sea-horses, and snake and sea-snails. There were baby sharks—one with a smile like a tiger.

Whilst we were having the run out in the car I noticed a man whose wife was apparently half-caste. I often wonder how a man like that feels, he is an absolute social outcast, as the Indians are too proud to mix with half-castes.

At night I went to the pictures, the seats are divided into two sections but there is no colour ban on either side. It was apparent that all the audience understood English.

Saturday

I hired a car for about two and a half hours and ran around the countryside, rather expensive at 30/-, but it is the only way to see anything. I took photographs of native boys spinning, washing banyan leaves, and even treading rice, also some photos of the water buffalo. I tasted some rice, and also ate a prickly pear—I was not too sucessful, getting a mouthful of prickles—it also had big pips but tasted sweet and very refreshing. They do not have red and yellow flowers growing together as I had thought, the flower is yellow and the fruit is red; the fruit can be cut by using one of the big spines of the leaf and so making a knife unnecessary.

Later I visited Saint Thomas's Mountain, there is a church on a hill about five miles from Madras, the view from there was wonderful. I saw both the government houses and both the forts.

The Theosophical Society is about five miles out of Madras, in the buildings I saw many ancient and curious documents and books, some written on rice-paper, others on palm leaves and all written in different languages. In the gardens I saw a wonderful banyan tree, the largest that I have ever seen. The gardens consist of about two hundred and thirty acres and in it reside the Theosophists of many faiths. One of the temples that I saw had an enormous terraced lake in front of it.

I am very glad that I came here, although I am still doubtful about the wisdom of going on. I am going anyway, and will try to forget the expense.

Hotel Bosotto,
Mount Road,
Madras.
10th February, 1928

Dear Harold and Gertrude,

I left Colombo on the evening of the 8th, and fortunately Mr. Carrodo de Mayla, Spaghetti, Cascara Jazgrada, or whatever you like to call him, was on the same train. Perhaps I had better explain—his correct name is the first one, and he is the Italian who travelled from Brisbane to Manila with us. He is quite a nice chap, although a bit excitable, he has been decent to me and I was only too glad to have someone to travel with in the train. I had expected him to go with me to Bombay tomorrow but he cannot, so I must go alone.

I'm afraid that you would get rather a shock at me wiring for more money so soon, but I had not reckoned on any expenses apart from the actual train and ferry travel from Colombo, through India and back to Colombo. To see anything of the places that I visit means hiring a car for a few hours, and the meals are extra on the train.

I had to buy bedding and also have a boy to look after my luggage, etc. He gets about 4/- per day which costs me about £6 for him as we will do about 200 hours of travel in the train. The boy is not an absolute necessity; but before starting I was given to understand that he was and that Europeans do not do such jobs as make their beds on the train. I could, of course, send him back now, but I would not get much refund on his ticket; it is booked on a sliding scale of a reduced fare for a greater mileage, and he is really quite useful if he looks after me as he should. All these little items add up so I though I had better get a bit of money in hand.

There is not time to write a long letter, in fact don't be surprised if you don't often hear from me for the next fortnight. In the train I find that I cannot write, and I have very little time out of it: when I have written a few postcards and made a few notes, I find that I am ready for a good night's rest.

Love from,
John.

P.S. Called at Binney's this morning to try to get in touch with Jim's brother and was very surprised to hear that he had gone home.

MADRAS TO BOMBAY

Sunday

I left Madras by train last night at nine o'clock and got put in with an objectionable Indian, but moved to another carriage. There were three of us in it; Chard, who hardly spoke at all; and Harley, a chap of about thirty-six, who was very talkative—he has a boy at school at Malvern, and the boy will be taking riding lessons from Hance later on.

The line first runs over a high plateau which was very uninteresting, then after the first few miles we passed fields of maize and prickly pear, and further up the line there were fields of cotton. The remainder of the crop of cotton looked rather poor, but judging by the number of bales at the station I should imagine that the picking season is over. I saw some sort of blaze and furore going on in a village at night. Driving the devil out of someone's house or body? The only other thing of interest was watching a native drinking; first he washed his mouth out, then he took a handful of water and washed his face, then he drank.

We have been travelling in the train for thirty-six hours. After leaving Poona in the early hours of the morning we are entering the Ghats, it is moonlight but the moon is not very strong. The countryside is very beautiful, but must be a thousand times more so by day, it is pretty cold as we are still 1,000 feet up.

The carriages are very large and comfortable, the sleeper has twin 6'6" beds with table in between, shower, w.c. and basin, and there is a good-size writing-table in the bedroom.

The hotels to stay at in Madras were the Cremana or Spencers, but not Bosettos, the food was quite good but the hotel was very dirty.

BOMBAY

At Bombay the place to stay is the Taj Mahal, but it is necessary to wire them a few days beforehand to book a room as it is very busy. I am staying at the Grand which is pretty hopeless, the food is not bad but it is not a very impressive place, the Majestic does not look too bad. The worst of it is that none of the hotels has a garden although in Madras Spencers Hotel had one. I forgot to mention that you should visit the Technical Institute in Madras.

If you buy anything here you will most assuredly get stung, which reminds me, beware of mosquitoes in Bombay as they are very malarial.

Bombay is a very impressive city, it is apparently well laid out, and possesses some very fine buildings. I visited the Hanging Gardens, the outlook is very nice, they consist of a garden of about eight acres and underneath it is an underground lake. When I got there I was rather disappointed as there was nothing to see; the Museum was not open, neither was the Tower of Silence. I went to the Burning Gardens, but will not do it again.

I saw the gateway to India, it is a very impressive piece of architecture and occupies a commanding position. We drove through the Victoria Park and saw the animals, a very fine lot they are. The market, or bazaar was perhaps the most interesting of all the places, with the pavement and the shops thronging with people of all castes. I was surprised at the enormous number of jewellers and silversmiths.

BOMBAY TO AGRA

I had the coupe to myself all the way. We left Bombay at 1.15 on Wednesday, and arrived at Agra at 4.15 on Thursday. It was hot but not unbearably so, cool towards the evening, and very cold at night. I must not again forget to lock the carriage door, I have just found it open, but have not lost anything.

What a wonderful difference irrigation makes to the land, there are many opportunities to see the comparisons from the train. I saw a new type of well with the buckets driven by oxen turning a capstan.

I am trying to see if the countryside is fairly well populated. At one time I counted about twenty people per minute on one side of the line alone, they were mostly doing agricultural work or else washing. The first few miles from Bombay the railway line ran through a cotton manufacturing area; it looked quite homelike with these sights, and the smell of the cloth market. I wish I could hear the sound of a shuttle again.

The run was interesting and was mostly through broken hilly country which was well watered. There was plenty of rice growing and the vegetation was semi-tropical, this soon gave way, however, to foliage of a colder climate. Different sorts of native dwellings can be seen all the way along the track, from quite passable brick or stone structures to mud huts, mud hives, and even worse than these, places with just a few palm leaves which were plaited together, keeping out neither heat, cold nor damp; the poor farmers apparently work hard from morning to night but seem to get nothing for it.

There were many temples, mosques, and other buildings to be seen, mostly built on high ground. The forts which could be seen from the train were in various states of decay. Gwalior has a remarkable fort built on a rock about 1,000 feet up, it is about three quarters of a mile long and tapers from eight to two hundred yards across; a most formidable place in ancient times, but apparently not so today.

THE TAJ MAHAL

A dream in marble

This must surely be the most beautiful building in the world, and when one considers the difficulties overcome in the building of it then it seems even more wonderful. It took 2,000 men eighteen years to build it, at a cost of £4,000,000. The beauty of it as a whole is absolutely indescribable, and then one sees the marvellous carvings and inlays. I visited the fort, and then the inside of the palace. Inside, almost the whole of the building the roofs and walls are carved, the most effective piece of work was the bathroom which had no light except candles; many of the walls of the palace are inlaid with glass, and when lit with candles and chandeliers it gives a most fabulous sparkling effect—no photos can do it justice.

In Agra I saw several weddings. I also heard the tale of the bull and the golden chain. There were many men to be seen working at their trades in the street—tailors sewing, potters at their wheels, bakers at the food shops; there were some masons at work in the street, building what looked like a grain store. There were a surprising number of smiths of all sorts working in silver, tin, brass, and base metals; I saw a trunk being made in leather, and its four metal clips being also made—it was quite cheap. I bought a 27″ brass tray which was quite reasonable. Up and down the road there were many water-carriers and also camels; you could see embrodiery being done in the shops, and ladies inspecting each others hair. At the barber's a cow was parked outside whilst the man had a shave; I saw a chair-maker at work using cane. Monkeys and cows seemed to be living in people's houses.

AGRA TO DELHI

20th February, 1928

It has been quite a decent run to Delhi, we left Agra at 4.40 and the train arrived at Delhi at about eight o'clock, a journey of about 120 miles. I saw the usual scenes, with the addition of the camel; also donkeys, which seem to be very popular up here. The birds were very striking, about a dozen peacocks were to be seen all together and many other brightly-coloured birds, there were also a few storks, they are perhaps the most graceful fliers that I have ever seen.

Delhi was very full, and it is almost impossible to get a room anywhere. I was fortunate enough to get a tent, it was about eighteen feet long and fifteen feet wide and was furnished with mats, a wardrobe, a dressing-table and bed, and was complete with a small dressing-room attached. It was quite comfortable but I was rather cold.

I visited a cotton mill quite accidentally. The bearer had suggested it, and thinking that it was just a hand-weaving place, I went. The mill secretary showed me round: as my guide knew hardly any English, and even less about the practical side of it, it was useless to try and get him to talk, I did, however, get to look right round the factory and saw practically everything.

I saw the full preparation of the cotton from its raw state for the first time, the women sit up amongst the unginned cotton and feed it into the machines by hand, which, by the way, appeared to be very old and primitive. Actually, to me the ginned cotton did not appear to be a great improvement on the unginned. Also in the preparation rooms were the carding machines from which the dust was just blowing into the open: the atmosphere in these rooms was filthy on account of the inefficiency, or lack of extractor fans.

In the spinning mill there were several open troughs which were about two feet square, apparently to hold water in hot weather. The floor was in a poor state of repair with several holes in it especially in dark corners. Most of the work was done on ring-spinners, there were just two sets of mule-spinners with several sets of rails running along the floor. Steam was injected into both the spinning and weaving rooms to keep them humid.

The weaving was done in the usual type of shed, the engines are by Shcultzer and by Nick Hargreaves, the looms by Hacking and there were also a few Austrian Prillers. They were only working two looms per person and there seemed to be dozens of hangers-on. The whole place would have been an eye-opener to Myers, or to any factory inspector, with the large number of workers milling about and the dirt and rubbish all over the place.

I saw round the bleaching and dyeing plant, and there was at least one machine for printing the cloth where necessary. In the dye shed the workers had no footwear whatever.

It is quite the most self-contained unit that I have ever seen, not only did the processes go right through from working the raw cotton ready for spinning, weaving, bleaching and dyeing and some printing of the cloth, but the mill was also equipped with its own foundry and workshop to cope with all this equipment. There must have been about 2,500 looms, and as many as 3,000 people employed here altogether. The whole factory must be fairly prosperous as it is being considerably extended.

I have to wait here in Delhi for another day before setting off for Calcutta, via Lucknow and Benares. To Calcutta will take about three days in the train.

The places to visit in Delhi are the fort, the mosque (where it is necessary to change your shoes), and the parliamentary buildings; one ought to see both the old and new cities, with the spire at the crossroads. The hotels to stay at are the Cecil and the Madras. To hire a car costs twenty-five rupees for a half day, a guide costs five rupees per day—mine was not worth it. The Ivory Palace was well worth a visit.

There is a lot of beautiful ivory work, and you can buy inlaid ivory boxes fairly cheaply near the Mosque, fifteen rupees for a small one. The Kashmir shawls near the fort were very dear, but you can get Kashmir shawls and embroidered work at the place opposite the Hotel Cecil.

Hotel Cecil,
Delhi.
20th February, 1928

Dear Reg,

I have been intending to write you a letter for weeks but I have not had much time, besides which the postcards which I have sent you can describe things far better than I can. I have forgotten both when I last wrote, and what I told you, but I don't think I have written to you since Singapore.

I had only a few days at Colombo and since then I have alternatively been travelling in the train nonstop for about thirty-six hours and then stopping for about forty-eight hours. The part of India around Delhi is the most interesting so far, at least it is for the tourist, as there is more to see in a smaller space.

The country in the south is tropical, and the vegetation consists of a great amount of cactus, palm and prickly pear amongst many other trees and shrubs, the names of which I don't know. Up here the more temperate trees grow, including the ash and the elm, and on the higher land all the English trees can be found. I have not been, nor shall I be able to go over any really hilly country. I should like to have seen something of it but there is no time.

Most of the countryside along the railway track is fairly well cultivated in a primitive sort of way, it looks as though if given proper scientific treatment it could prove very fertile, but the natives will never change and will keep on with their old methods of farming.

It is very interesting to see the country life of the people and quite a lot can be seen from the train. Many villages have been built near the old forts, they are system built in a sort of brick, just hovels of only one storey, they have no windows or doors, only holes. Those built for the railway people are slightly better, they are mostly of brick but don't keep out the wet. Some of their mud huts are more like ant-hills and are not even big enough to stand up in. Perhaps the worst dwellings are those made of palm or other leaves, as they keep out neither the rain, frost or sun.

Often one sees a cow lying across the doorway, in fact, they even get inside the houses as they are sacred to the Hindu and are left to do as they please. I have often seen them lying across the footpaths here in Delhi and no one moves them.

The people are always dirty, although their religion forces them to bathe and to wash their mouths once a day, how dirty they get after that does not seem to matter. They are, however, pretty clean feeders and their bowls and brass vessels are kept beautifully clean.

Some of the old forts and palaces are very beautiful, many of the forts are really like walled cities; the best preserved ones that I have seen are at Gwalior, Agra and Delhi: the one at Gwalior was particularly interesting as it is built on a hill something the size of Pendle but far steeper, the fort itself is almost inaccessible.

The most beautiful building by far is the Taj Mahal at Agra, I have a few photos of it but they don't do it justice, the only way to appreciate it is to see it for yourself.

I think you will probably be more interested in all the different animals that I have seen. Once, along the railway, I thought I saw a couple of wolves but I am not sure, they did not really look like dogs, even alsatians especially when they moved. I have seen scores of monkeys, it is not unusual for them to be playing about at the stations, often coming down and sitting on the carriage roofs to be fed. Another animal to be seen everywhere is a tiny squirrel with black or dark brown stripes, he has a long and very bushy tail, when he stands still the tail is horizontal, but he seems to be unable to move without it bobbing up, he is very quick a "wick 'un", but he is not at all timid.

Yesterday I saw a mongoose—that is not the masculine of goose! It was like a cross between a large rat and a small badger and was also very "wick". I have seen many more strange animals but as they were all caged they are not worth describing to you.

In Madras I visited the aquarium, it was quite the most wonderful that I have ever seen, there were fish of every shape and colour imaginable and unimaginable, from perfect globular ones to almost square ones; there were fish that climb as well as swim.

It is possible to see many kinds of brightly coloured birds from the train but the only one that I recognize are the parrots, storks, cranes and peacocks. I saw a dozen of the latter all at once from the train on Friday.

Many different sorts of animals are used here for transport, mostly donkeys, mules, cattle of various kinds, and up here the camel. There are not many horses about, they are used principally for riding and for drawing tongas (which is a two-wheeled trap built very low) and gharries (which are like our English victorias).

The donkeys and mules are normally used to draw loads on carts and to carry goods, they often carry such a load that it is impossible to distinguish the animal from the goods—especially if the latter happens to be mud pies which the natives use for fuel. Oxen are used for all purposes; ploughing, which consists of only two pieces of wood, one horizontal and one upright and with the ploughman's weight behind, also for rolling corn or rice, and operating wells.

Some of the wells are operated by the oxen giving a direct pull on the rope, others by a sort of capstan working on a wheel with buckets on it.

The rice has to be separated from the ears by rolling it, (if you open the ears you will see the seeds of rice inside). On the farm the ears of rice are first separated from their stems by allowing the oxen to trample on them. The rice is then put in a circular trough (which may have been used to grind corn or even to mix mortar), the roller is then pulled round and round by the oxen.

The carts used here are of all descriptions, many have sides just made of rope stretched over a wooden frame. Quite often a camel is to be seen carrying a huge load, and occasionally pulling a great cumbersome four-wheeled cart.

These things, as you can imagine, are all very fascinating and I suppose you will be wanting to come and see them for yourself. I am now very glad that I came up here and did not spend all my time in Ceylon.

It will not be long before I set off for home now. After I have seen Calcutta I will be retracing my journey back to Ceylon.

I hope you are keeping well, and having a good time.

Cheerio,

John.

P.S. I have packed some rice away in my trunk so will bring it along home with me. I enclose a quick sketch of the simple wooden plough.

EPILOGUE

So we are left wondering what effect the world trip had on young John Hindley both personally, and with regard to what he had found out about the textile trade within the Empire.

Certainly the travelling had widened his horizons, and also had increased his confidence. My father always said that he loved sailing. I remember that he was always fascinated by any sort of shipping vessel. He rarely spoke of his travels to us as children, however, perhaps we just never asked.

It would be nice to think that what he saw and heard on his travels had some bearing on what happened in subsequent years at the mill. I think that in some small ways it did, as although at boardroom level he was always treated very much as the youngest brother, yet as regards the day to day working of the mill, he never lost his personal touch.

Perhaps the most important thing that he had learned was that the export trade to the rest of the world from Britain, was on the decline. If this encouraged his belief in the need for progress and expansion in the home market, with the need to experiment with new methods and fibres, then the trip had been well worthwhile.

As has been already mentioned, John came back to troubled times. The Depression was to hit the textile industry, and by 1939 the whole industry employed half the number of people that it had done in 1913. The worst hit towns were those where, together with allied trades, the weaving of cloth was the only form of employment. During this time over 800 mills in Lancashire were closed, making a quarter of a million people jobless. Japan was filling the gap in world trade for the demand for cloth, and it was being made at one fifth of the Lancashire wages.

In 1938 there was a strike of the tacklers (foreman) at Bankfield Mill, the cause was said to be that a tackler struck a weaver—others said the reverse—but wherever the truth lay it was probably sparked off by an undercurrent of dissatisfaction and anxiety on both sides. Although wages were appallingly low by modern standards, those in Nelson were the highest in Lancashire at 35/7½d per week, the lowest being at Wigan at 23/11d. There was no minimum wage, and as weavers were paid by the number of looms worked, if orders fell off the number of working looms was reduced; weavers could also be fined for any fault in the cloth, it could be disputed as to whether this had been caused by faulty yarn or faulty machinery, rather than by the weaver's poor workmanship.

Another cause of unrest was the "more looms system" manufacturers, who did have full order books, strove to increase efficiency by an increase in the number of looms per worker as machinery became more automated: but the operatives saw this move as a threat of unemployment to the majority.

Through a combination of favourable conditions in Nelson, technical skills, good management within the mill, and astute direction in finance from Harold, the firm was able to survive these troubled times.

One interesting development of this period was the growth of the multiple stores and their sale of garments. I would guess from the writings in the diary, that Harold had told his youngest brother John, to call on such stores in Sydney and other major Australian towns to see what they had to offer. Harold subsequently took a great interest in these large multiples and became a director of British Home Stores in 1935. He was canny enough to be hedging his bets, since, although the stores would buy cloth at prices below those at Hindley Bros. were prepared to sell, he could see that if the price of finished garments fell drastically it would be the multiple stores that would make a profit. Another cousin, Derek Cornes, remembers Harold giving him a £5 note for pocket money—a considerable sum to a school boy in those days. He was told to go to the nearby newly-opened British Home Stores in York to see what it was like to buy whatever he fancied.

Not only was machinery improving technically, but so was the adequate provision of light and power. Expensive automated looms need to be run at maximum capacity, and so the idea of shift—and possibly of night-work was mooted: this idea did not go down well in Lancashire, and so the firm expanded into Yorkshire, and went on to weaving worsted cloths and suiting in Bradford.

Now all that has gone. The weaving sheds at Bankfield have been flattened to provide car parking; some buildings are used as an office.

The New Mill at Bradford is used for making electronics, whilst the original sturdy Bankfield Mill, built in 1895, lies empty. Within less than a century a whole era has come and gone.

The letters from Jim Cunliffe who became mill foreman, and later manager, and from Albert Aspinall who was to sell much of the modern machinery to Hindley Bros., are also able to put on record what actually happened after my fathers world trip.

(Letter from Jim Cuncliffe to V. Cutter 20/8/84 continued)

I remember your father's return from his world trip quite well, because it was after he returned, when changes began to take place in the mill. He certainly came back with modern ideas of running the business.

In early thirties we branched out into weaving ray-de-chines and crepe-de-chines, using an artificial silk weft. This proved a difficult period owing to the handling of the yarn; which was so very lively, that it caused many problems. But, eventually these were overcome, and very soon being handled as well as ordinary cotton.

As the quality of yarn and warps were improved, and the handling of the same, it became obvious that more looms could be run per weaver.

Mr. John was a great advocate of the more looms system, and it was introduced under great opposition from the weavers' union. After a period of dissention, soon the weavers were working six, and eight looms, and later twelve looms each.

During the Second World War we were switched over to government work, which meant weaving cloths for the Army and Air Force. Cloths for uniforms, overalls, etc. We also wove specialized nylon cloth for parachutes. All these cloths were subject to government inspection which was of a very high standard.

After the war we continued to develop the nylon trade, making fabrics for underwear, dresses shirtings, etc. for such firms as Marks and Spencers.

A period I clearly remember was the overlookers strike at the mill in about 1938, when all the union men were sacked and the firm decided to train their own men. During this time the brothers, particularly John, came quite regularly in the evenings to help out, and worked with the foreman and the managers of that time.

Another thing I remember about Harold and John was that most Saturday mornings they would walk round the mill in either plus-fours and sports jacket, or riding gear, johdpurs, etc., according to what sport they were taking part in on that particular day. Of course mills used to work on Saturday mornings until 11.00 a.m. in those days.

On most days during the week Mr. John would walk round the mill, and anything that he saw that displeased him was recorded and a note would be on my desk for my attention.

You will be aware of subsequent progress after the merger with

Samuel Holden, then Carrington Dewhurst, Vyella, etc.

These are just some rambling memories as I have thought of them, but I hope that you may be able to glean something from them which may be of help to you about those early days.

Yours,

James Cunliffe.

*   *   *

(Letter from Albert Aspinall to V. Cutter 28/12/83)

I took the Crompton and Knowles agency in 1936 and began to peddle automatic looms, but it was 1945 before I broke the ice at Bankfield.

That year—or was it 1946—the British Rayon Weavers' Association (of Manchester) was encouraged by the government to send a team to the U.S.A. to learn the developments of the American textile industry that had been made during the war, and to study their methods of production. The team included your father, Johnnie Duckworth, Stanley Emmott (of Cowling) and a male secretary; the team was lead by Mr. Joe Nelson*.

I was invited by Crompton and Knowles to be available at their works at Worcester (Massachusetts) to meet the team, and was subsequently seconded to them for a grand tour of the mills, especially those in the south, i.e. in Carolina.

Your father and I by that time were good friends. I had already had the good luck to introduce a modern method of winding (Swiss Schweiters) which had helped to increase the number of looms per weaver.

After our tour—all went out by sea and back, as no air travel was available then—Hindleys decided to try out the Crompton and Knowles S6 automatic loom. A small order for 24 was placed and the looms ultimately installed at Bankfield.

Nelson at that time was known as Little Moscow, there was no, or very little, co-operation from the tacklers or weavers during the trials.

This resistance proved too much for Hindley Bros. who decided to build a mill at Horton Bank Top—a suburb of Bradford. The City of Bradford co-operated by building new houses for the mill operatives.

*Son of Sir Amos Nelson.

We installed some automatic looms, and the trials, in spite of some opposition in operation, were a success.

The looms were delivered and installed during 1947-48-49. The Marshall-Aid Plan, which was set up directly after the war by the U.S.A government gave assistance with extremely good credit terms between the nations involved (not individuals). As far as I was concerned, the looms were rationed and sold on a quota delivery basis. In one way this was a good thing, because the change-over to automatic weaving at the mill was thus a gradual process—but to me it was lousy because I had to wait so long for our commission!

Finally—your question about world trade in the period I have written about. All I can say is that it was a near boom period for the textile industry; and your family business was one of the leading successes in their particular field during this time. But now, alas, what a sad change to an almost impotent industry as far as Lancashire is concerned. How many mills are there in Nelson today? Blackburn had 120 mills when I was a young man, today it has two.

Yours,
Albert.

Background Reading

Lancashire, D. H. Marshall.
Lancashire Under The Hammer, Bowker (Published 1927).
The Economics of Man-made Fibres, Douglas C. Hague.
Burnley Chamber of Commerce 1927 Journal.
Nelson Textile Society 1914 Journal.
The Lancashire Textile Industry, Pocket edition 1932.
Industrial Lancashire in 1897, J. Mortimer.
A Brief History of Lancashire, McIntyre (Published 1923).
New Fields for Industry in 1955, North East Lancs. Journal.

QUOTATIONS

R1—*Lancashire,* D. H. Marshall.
R2—*Nanking Road,* Vicki Baum.